I Became Alone

Five Women Poets

JUDITH THURMAN

I Became Alone

Five Women Poets

Sappho

Louise Labé

Ann Bradstreet

Juana Ines de la Cruz

Emily Dickinson

Decorations by James and Ruth McCrea

ATHENEUM   New York   1975

for Alice, Arkie and Eva

Library of Congress Cataloging in Publication Data

Thurman, Judith,   I became alone.
SUMMARY: Explores five women poets, ranging from Sappho to
Emily Dickinson, through brief biographies and selections of
their poetry. 1. Women poets—Juvenile literature. 2. Women's
writings. [1. Poets. 2. Women — Biography. 3. Women's writ-
ings] I. McCrea, James. II. McCrea, Ruth. III. Title.
PN471.T5   808.81   75-9589
ISBN 0-689-30487-0

The poems of Sappho are reprinted from *Sappho: A New Trans-
lation*, translated by Mary Barnard, originally published by the
University of California Press; reprinted by permission of The
Regents of the University of California.

Stanzas from "Describes Rationally the Irrational Effects of
Love," reprinted from *An Anthology of Mexican Poetry*, compiled by Octavio Paz, translated by Samuel Beckett. Copyright
© 1958 by Indiana University Press, Bloomington, Reprinted by
permission of the publisher.

Contents

Preface

*W*omen today have a passionate interest in each other's work, and I think this has always been true. Sappho schooled young girls in poetry and music; Louise Labé dedicated her book to her young protégée; Emily Dickinson's favorite writer was George Eliot[1]—and so was Gertrude Stein's when she was young. Whenever a contemporary poet like Adrienne Rich or Elizabeth Bishop gives a reading, the hall is crowded with women listening.

What makes women's writing so urgent and compelling for other women? A modern poet, Laura Riding, has written: "There is something to be told about us for the telling of which we all wait . . . Until the missing story of ourselves is told, nothing besides told can suffice us: we shall go on quietly craving it."

Great writers, most of whom have been men, have written indelibly about women. But it is not just portraits, heroines, or even truths about ourselves that we lack. Part of what we crave "to be told about us" is that we are creators. We want to identify not only with the characters and feelings of a work of art, but with its greatness, with the act of telling, itself.

For that reason, women who have been creators are of great consequence to us. They have been rare, for until recently we have been begrudged the fair chance to become artists. Like the American frontierswomen, who made their wonderful patchworks from scraps of sacking and used cloth, women writers have often worked from material gleaned and hoarded in moments borrowed from other duties, in moments when no one was looking. They have argued and intrigued for their privacy and their education. They have sometimes used men's names or worn men's clothes in order to be heard seriously—without prejudice or condescension. And sometimes they have had to forfeit the respect of others—even family and friends—in order to redeem themselves as artists. For people have feared a woman's imagination, her power—independently—to give life.

The five poets in this book come from vastly different cultures and centuries. They offer us a sampler of women's most traditional roles: wife, mother, nun, spinster, and "other woman"—woman of the world. Their styles are distinct, and so is what they tell us about living.

But had they been able to meet in person, as we meet them in this book, I think they would have recognized what, as women, unites them—and why their poetry has survived. Central to each one was her identity as a creator—an identity that put her whole life into focus, into relief, a relief like the italics of a text. *Feeling an inner happiness,* says Louise Labé . . . *Becoming oneself,* says Emily Dickinson . . . *Creating something uniquely one's own,* says Anne Bradstreet . . . and Juana Ines, *loyally obliging one's own nature.* For Sappho, who had the fewest obstacles and probably the greatest talent, writing meant defining, revealing, relishing herself in her poems—a self she believed, correctly, would be "immortal."

If we read their work because they are women, we also read it because it is good poetry—good in the absolute, not good "for women." Quality has no gender: there are no "poetesses." These five poets wrote, and are, for everyone.

JUDITH THURMAN

Sappho

Although they are

Only breath, words
which I command
are immortal.

Our knowledge of Sappho is as sparse, precious and tantalizing as the debris from a dead planet. We are told by Plato[2] and others she was the greatest woman of her time, one of the great poets of all time. But the early Christians burned her books, and from that loss scholars have been able to recover only a handful of poems. They have found a few lines quoted as examples—and so preserved—by ancient critics and grammarians. They have rescued poems from papyri that had been torn into strips and used for stuffing mummies. The earliest fragment of Sappho's work was discovered on the shard of an old jar. We can only guess at that jar's shape, like the true shape of the poems—and at how much they once contained.

Sappho was born about 620 B.C., some say in Mytelene and some in Eresus on the Greek island of Lesbos. She lived at the same time as Aesop, the fabulist, as the prophet Jeremiah, as Solon the Athenian lawgiver. King Croesus was amassing his legendary wealth in Lydia, just across the Aegean Sea. Nebuchadnezzar was conquering Jerusalem.[3]

Lesbos was and still is one of the loveliest Aegean islands. It is balder today than in Sappho's time; goats and shipbuilders have cropped its grasses and trees. Then it was

(Sappho is pronounced: SAF-foe)

covered with vineyards, with groves of apples and olives. On the hillsides there were waterfalls, on the cliffs, wildflowers.

In the sixth century B.C., Lesbos was a center of culture and trade, famous for its wine and poetry. Sappho wrote that the poets of Lesbos "tower above all others." Thirty years before her birth, her countryman, Terpander, had invented the seven-string lyre, and with it, the tradition of lyric song.

We presume Sappho's family was rich and noble, for when the nobility lost its power to a popular dictator[4] and many aristocrats were exiled, Sappho was among them. She was exiled twice, we think, and probably lived for a while in Syracuse, a thriving colony on the coast of Sicily, which was becoming the New York of its day. Each of her exiles ended with an amnesty, and she was allowed to return home. But although it appears she was involved, at least indirectly, in politics she never writes about them. She shuns heroism, issues, events, exploits, and looks inward to the feelings and details harbored by a private life.

Very little is certain about Sappho's family. Her father's name was Scamandronymous. Her mother was called Cleis, and Sappho gave her mother's melodious name to her own child. Sappho and her mother were both black-haired, perhaps with olive skins and dark eyes. We know as much because she says so in a poem: "We were dark," she tells her child. But little Cleis was fair—"like a golden flower." Sappho swears she "wouldn't take all Croesus' kingdom with love thrown in, for her."

It seems that Sappho was married to a businessman from

the island of Andros. His name was Cercolas. Perhaps he died, or perhaps they lived apart—Sappho never refers to him in her poems. We know she had two brothers. Charaxus, the elder, was a rich wine merchant and something of a playboy. Sappho scolds him for eloping with a famous courtesan, and he seems to have told her she was a nuisance. Their younger brother, Larychus, was an official cup-bearer who served wine to guests at state banquets. It was an office kept for the noblest and most virtuous young boys.

We don't know what Sappho looked like, except by hearsay. Alcaeus, her fellow poet, who seems to have been in love with her, calls her "violet-haired, holy, and sweetly smelling Sappho." Strabo, a Roman writing 500 years after her death, when the body of her work was still intact, knew enough to call her "a miracle of a young woman." But, also, we are told that she was "small and dark like a nightingale, with unshapely wings enfolding a tiny body." A modern writer[5] puzzling over these conflicting descriptions, suggests that perhaps she was, like a great actress, able to project the illusion of being beautiful—an illusion animated by "grace, timing, spirit."

Her character is vivid in her poems. She claims to have "a childlike heart," and she has a child's capacity for being serious, stubborn, and inspired. She is equally greedy and generous with her love. She enjoys a drama, especially when she is the center of it. Her wit sometimes has a cruel taste; she scorns clumsiness, ugliness, anything she considers vulgar. Yet for all her greatness and *finesse,* Sappho is never a snob. She understands by feeling—especially by feeling pain. Her poetry is humbly honest about those feelings.

Sappho's poems were known by heart throughout Greece. Solon, himself, the ruler of Athens, wanted to learn one on his deathbed. Aristotle[6] tells us she was honored by her fellow citizens. "The wise are honored universally . . . and the Mytelenes honored Sappho for all she was a woman."

"For all she was a woman" was Aristotle's way of saying she was honored in spite of being a lowly woman. For by his time, about 350 B.C., the status of women in Greece had been degraded. Their lives were separate from their men's, who dined, played music, discussed philosophy, and even loved in a society that excluded women. But in Sappho's day, especially on the island of Lesbos, women enjoyed great freedom and were important members of the community. There were a number of women poets besides Sappho;[7] they presided at religious festivals for which they also wrote and performed songs.

Sappho's household was dedicated to the arts of music and poetry. She calls it *moisopolon domos*, "the house of those who cultivate the Muses."[8] She shared her daily life with a group of young women who came to her from all parts of Greece and Asia Minor—girls from noble families whose parents apparently paid for them to study with her until it was time to marry. An ancient critic noted that "they come from Miletus, from Phocaea, from Colophon to live in Sappho's society, and one day they go away again."

There are serious theories and much gossip about Sappho's relations with those young women. One scholar[9] believes that Sappho was the head or priestess of a *thiasos*, a college of women bound to each other by religious vows who worshiped Aphrodite—the goddess of love[9a]—cared for her temple, and performed at her public rituals. Another scholar[10] thinks the idea of a "school" or "convent" is unlikely, and that Sappho's disciples were, like those of Socrates,[11] attracted by the glamour of her genius. A modern translator of Sappho's poems[12] makes a different analogy. She suggests that Sappho was like a Renaissance master with a studio of apprentice painters. "For some reason people thought it advisable for young women to study and practice the composition of poetry and music . . ." In Sparta, a poet named Alcman "trained and wrote for choruses of girls . . . and we have good reason to assume that Sappho performed the same service for her native city . . . The parents of ambitious young girls who aspired to the position might, in that case, have been moved to send them to study with the most celebrated lyricist of the day if she were willing to accept them as students, companions, apprentices, novices, or whatever word may be considered appropriate."

Sappho calls the young girls "comrades," but it seems clear that among them she found lovers as well as friends and apprentices. It is as an aroused lover that she writes about their beauty and her own longing for it. The word "Lesbian"—someone from the island of Lesbos—pays hommage to Sappho and has come to mean women who are lovers of other women.

Sappho's love of women did not exclude love of men. As she aged her dark hair whitened; her eyes probably became more and more luminous, taking on the burden of her beauty. Like other brilliant and great women—Queen Elizabeth the First, George Eliot—she seems to have attracted much younger men. "Of course I love you," she promises one suitor, "but if you love me, marry a young woman."

Her own aging was very poignant to her. Once, thinking she is near death, she warns her daughter Cleis that sounds of grief are unbecoming in a poet's household. In another poem she is tired, alone in bed; she wants to die, to "open like a lotus."

There is a romantic legend that Sappho, at fifty, fell madly in love with Phaon, a young ferryman. She pursued him all over Greece and when he finally rebuffed her, she threw herself from the Leucadian Cliffs.[13] But this story is hard to believe—not only because we have no proof, but because Sappho's footing in life, her sense of grace, was too firm for such a fall.

I have no complaint

Prosperity that
the golden Muses
gave me was no
delusion; dead, I
won't be forgotten.

Sappho spoke and wrote in the soft Aeolian dialect,[14] and probably pronounced her name "Psappha." Her poems belong to the "lyric" tradition. Today "lyric" has two meanings, both derived from the original Greek use of the word. "Lyrics" are the words that accompany a tune. And "lyric poetry" refers to short poems whose subjects are personal and intensely felt. Sappho's "lyrics" were sung to the accompaniment of a lyre. She herself invented a twenty-stringed lyre, and a *pectis,* or small harp. She played and sang her own poems, and perhaps for this reason we have such an intimate sense of her voice, reading them. Eventually they were taught to professional singers, who performed them all over Greece.

Before her work was destroyed by the early Christians, who thought it was obscene, it consisted of nine books—epigrams, elegies, wedding songs, and songs for one voice. She probably wrote on commission—religious hymns paid for by the state, and wedding songs for wealthy clients. We don't know what the music was like, but when the ancients write of Sappho, they describe a marriage of sense and sound unrivaled in Greek poetry.

Unless a desert shifts, and some buried city yields us an ancient library, we can't put Sappho together—we can only cherish the pieces. Even these pieces have been frustrating and expensive to recover. Many of the original poems were copied into rolls of papyrus, which, in the course of centuries, were torn into strips and used for other purposes—used, for example, to mummify royal crocodiles. One line of a poem will turn up inside a mummy. Perhaps another will be found quoted in an ancient grammar, or fired into the glaze of an old piece of pottery, an urn or jar. Fitting together those blasted bits has involved immense scholarship, immense patience—and some bold guesswork.

It is tempting to finish the unfinished, to make an "artist's version" of a ruined city or a text. Many of Sappho's translators have tried to remake her. They have roofed, plastered, and furnished her poems from their own stores, leaving no feeling of the life they once housed.

But Mary Barnard, whose translations follow, brings a new respect for the authentic—and for the mysterious. She also has a modern sympathy for Sappho's honesty about her feelings. The Sappho that follows is what she said in her own words, or "what they say she said."[14a]

7

At noontime

When the earth is
bright with flaming
heat falling straight down

the cricket sets
up a high-pitched
singing in his wings

I took my lyre and said:

Come now, my heavenly
tortoise shell: become
a speaking instrument

Although they are

Only breath, words
which I command
are immortal

17

Sleep, darling

I have a small
daughter called
Cleis, who is

like a golden
flower
        I wouldn't
take all Croesus'
kingdom with love
thrown in, for her

83

Don't ask me what to wear

I have no embroidered
headband from Sardis to
give you, Cleis, such as
I wore
            and my mother
always said that in her
day a purple ribbon
looped in the hair was thought
to be high style indeed

but we were dark:
                        a girl
whose hair is yellower than
torchlight should wear no
headdress but fresh flowers

44

Without warning

As a whirlwind
swoops on an oak
Love shakes my heart

38

Prayer to my lady of Paphos

Dapple-throned Aphrodite,
eternal daughter of God,
snare-knitter! Don't, I beg you,

cow my heart with grief! Come,
as once when you heard my far-
off cry and, listening, stepped

from your father's house to your
gold car, to yoke the pair whose
beautiful thick-feathered wings

oaring down mid-air from heaven
carried you to light swiftly
on dark earth; then, blissful one,

smiling your immortal smile
you asked, What ailed me now that
made me call you again? What

was it that my distracted
heart most wanted? "Whom has
Persuasion to bring round now

"to your love? Who, Sappho, is
unfair to you? For, let her
run, she will soon run after;

"if she won't accept gifts, she
will one day give them; and if
she won't love you—she soon will

"love, although unwillingly. . . ."
If ever—come now! Relieve
this intolerable pain!

What my heart most hopes will
happen, make happen; you your-
self join forces on my side!

37

You know the place: then

Leave Crete and come to us
waiting where the grove is
pleasantest, by precincts

sacred to you; incense
smokes on the altar, cold
streams murmur through the

apple branches, a young
rose thicket shades the ground
and quivering leaves pour

down deep sleep; in meadows
where horses have grown sleek
among spring flowers, dill

scents the air. Queen! Cyprian!*
Fill our gold cups with love
stirred into clear nectar

---

* Aphrodite

39

He is more than a hero

He is a god in my eyes—
the man who is allowed
to sit beside you—he

who listens intimately
to the sweet murmur of
your voice, the enticing

laughter that makes my own
heart beat fast. If I meet
you suddenly, I can't

speak—my tongue is broken;
a thin flame runs under
my skin; seeing nothing,

hearing only my own ears
drumming, I drip with sweat;
trembling shakes my body

and I turn paler than
dry grass. At such times
death isn't far from me

43

It was you, Atthis, who said

"Sappho, if you will not get
up and let us look at you
I shall never love you again!

"Get up, unleash your suppleness,
lift off your Chian nightdress
and, like a lily leaning into

"a spring, bathe in the water.
Cleis is bringing your best
purple frock and the yellow

"tunic down from the clothes chest;
you will have a cloak thrown over
you and flowers crowning your hair . . .

"Praxinoa, my child, will you please
roast nuts for our breakfast? One
of the gods is being good to us:

"today we are going at last
into Mitylene, our favorite
city, with Sappho, loveliest

"of its women; she will walk
among us like a mother with
all her daughters around her

"when she comes home from exile . . ."

But you forget everything

50

But you, monkey face

Atthis, I loved you
long ago while you
still seemed to me a
small ungracious child

I was proud of you, too

In skill I think
you need never
bow to any girl

not one who may
see the sunlight
in time to come

After all this

Atthis, you hate
even the thought

of me. You dart
off to Andromeda*

---

* Sappho's rival

42

I have had not one word from her

Frankly I wish I were dead.
When she left, she wept

a great deal; she said to
me, "This parting must be
endured, Sappho. I go unwillingly."

I said, "Go, and be happy
but remember (you know
well) whom you leave shackled by love

"If you forget me, think
of our gifts to Aphrodite
and all the loveliness that we shared

"all the violet tiaras,
braided rosebuds, dill and
crocus twined around your young neck

"myrrh poured on your head
and on soft mats girls with
all that they most wished for beside them

"while no voices chanted
choruses without ours,
no woodlot bloomed in spring without song . . ."

87

We know this much

Death is an evil;
we have the gods'
word for it; they too
would die if death
were a good thing

64

Tonight I've watched

The moon and then
the Pleiades*
go down

The night is now
half-gone; youth
goes; I am

in bed alone

---

*See page 139, note 16.

Louise Labé

"... a woman committing her ideas
to writing should be meticulous,
and not disdain glory."

Louise Labé is one of France's great lyric poets. She lived in Lyon during the high Renaissance, which took place from about 1520 to 1560. When she was born, in 1522, the stiff bodice of medieval life had been undone. Men and women were beginning to breathe and to aspire —not upward anymore, like their steep cathedrals—but to a new thoroughness of experience. Louise embodied these new appetites and hopes: to possess, to know, to invent, to excel, and to be remembered.

The "humanism" of the Renaissance was not humane. It was financed, in part, by bloodshed and labor which brought no return to those who had furnished them. But it did happen that more people were looking at the world curiously and not turning away from what they saw. Painters had come down from the scaffolding in the churches; they were painting real bodies, real scenes. In Lyon, a doctor named François Rabelais was writing about food, politics, and sex in prose so ripe you felt you could touch and smell the world of his stories.

During Louise's lifetime, Lyon was a crossroads for the armies and caravans returning to France from Italy and Germany. It was a free port for spices and luxuries from the Orient, the center of the silk trade and of the new industry

---

Labé is pronounced: lah-BAY

of printing. There were more than 400 printing presses in Lyon, and they were producing books of all kinds—Greek and Latin classics, newly rediscovered, and the newly created literature of the Renaissance. Royalty patronized the city; the court was a hub for the arts. Queen Marguerite of Navarre, herself a poet, gathered poets around her.

Louise's father had become rich during the boom. He was a ropemaker who had surfaced from his modest workshop on a back street to become a man of possessions and power. His name was Pierre Charly, but he was called Labé after one of his properties. He had a talent for outliving wives. He married three times, and each wife brought and left him a bigger fortune. Louise's mother was the second Madame Charly, Etienette Compagnon.

Like many newly rich men, Charly had lavish ambitions for his children. His sons were to be soldiers and his only daughter a distinguished lady; she would be educated like an Italian princess.

In one of her poems Louise proudly tells us that "I trained my wits, my body, and my mind with a thousand ingenious works." She was taught to embroider and to play the lute, to read Latin and Italian. But maybe because she had no mother to enforce decorum, she also learned to ride with her brothers, to throw a lance, to handle a pike, a war axe, to shoot a bow, and wield a dagger. She fought in tournaments and even, it is said, in a war. There is a legend that "Captain" Louise appeared in armor at the battle of Perpignan,[15] and met the future king of France, with whom she had a brief adventure.

If she was in love with the king, she regretted being so. She tells us that falling in love interfered with her sports and her studies. She had no more time for them when, at sixteen, love "seized my heart." Perhaps this explains her grudge against King Henri II, and why she pointedly refused to join his official welcome when he visited Lyon. From what she tells us in her poems—and from what she leaves out—we can guess that Louise Labé was a woman experienced in suffering—impulsive, proud, carnal, and self-aware. And that experience gave the same qualities to her writing.

In 1554, Louise, then twenty-two was married to Ennemond Perrin, her father's friend, a man more than thirty years older than she. He was, like her father, an artisan with a large and new fortune. It is hard to see the dazzling Louise willingly become Madame Perrin, wife of an old ropemaker. She never took her husband's name. They had no children. And yet their marriage was not the cruel joke it may have seemed. Perrin's existence gave her unusual freedom. Generously, or maybe helplessly, he made no demands on her. He left her the time to write, the means to live well, and the protection she needed to be herself—alone and intimately with others.

Louise's poetry and her life suggest she had a vitality as striking as her celebrated beauty. We can imagine her as a straight figure on a disciplined, sleek horse. We can see her inspecting her garden, snapping a leaf from the bay tree and bruising it to release the smell; a woman with an agile glance, a fencer's quickness in her step. And yet the one portrait of Louise made in her lifetime doesn't convey that power. It shows a woman with pretty, delicate features, light, curly hair, a half-smile, pursed and even slightly suspicious. We are told Louise hated it.

She spent her mornings at her "honest pastime": writing. Later, her friends came, and they stayed into the evening. Louise had a *salon;* her house was a gathering place for the literary figures of Lyon, a place where they drank and dined, intrigued, shared, and argued their ideas.

She wrote, she said, because it left her "happy within myself," and, too, because she liked to reread, to go back to the person she had been, to the places and feelings she had once lived:

> we recover the pleasure we have had in what we have written about it, or in the intelligence and analysis that we have acquired in the process—and beyond that, in the act of judgment, which forms and informs our fertile ideas, from the beginning, giving us a unique happiness.

Louise's only book was published on August 12, 1555, by the printer Jean de Tournes. It sold briskly enough to be reprinted the next year in two more editions, corrected by the author.

The book contained twenty-five sonnets, three longer poems (elegies) and a prose discourse—all "the work of my youth." She had not intended to publish it, but her friends warned her that a false or careless version of her poems could be pirated and sold without her permission.

Many great women have written about the men they love, while really addressing that experience to other women. Louise, too, wrote her poetry to a man, and dedicated it to a woman: Clémence de Bourges of Lyon. She was a nobleman's daughter, a girl of twenty whom Louise had great hopes for as a writer. "Because women don't willingly show themselves alone in public, I have chosen you to act as my guide," Louise told her. "I dedicate and send you this book with no other aim than to affirm the friendship I have, for a long time, felt for you, and to inspire you, seeing how crude and badly made my work is, to bring forth another, more finely tooled, and of better grace."

Louise had, though, another reason to invoke Clémence. She hoped Clémence's respectability would shield her from critics. For she knew her book would startle, embarrass, and threaten many people. The daring of her writing was like the physical courage of her girlhood, a desire "to equal or surpass men."

"I can do no better thing," she assured Clémence, "than to implore all virtuous women to raise their wits above their spindles and distaffs, and use those wits to make the world understand that if we are not fit to command, then we are not worthy to be companions of those who command and are obeyed."

Louise's book appeared at a time when most poets were writing about love. And most poets were men. Women were the subjects of poems, but they had no voice in them, except, perhaps, the voice their lovers ascribed to them.

An Italian, Francesco Petrarch, had set the standard for

most of the love poetry of the Renaissance. He invented a new form, the sonnet, a poem with fourteen lines and a strict rhyme scheme. Petrarch's sonnets were inspired by a remote, pure, and hard-to-believe woman whose name was Laura. They contained ornate descriptions of her beauty, and of the poet's pain: he desired her, but she always remained unreachable.

There were other poets, in France, contemporaries of Louise,[16] who were trying to write poetry closer to the real unruliness of love. But they were men, and could experiment in the safety of being men. No "decent" woman could publicly admit to having the ardor or experience necessary to write honestly about love. She had to pretend she was like Laura as Petrarch imagined her: indifferent to desire.

It was the unstinted and real feeling of Louise's poems that made them seem bold. She gave the woman in Renaissance poetry a believable woman's voice. That woman was not a symbol or a man's idea. She behaved in love with a passionate identity of her own.

Predictably, when her book appeared it caused a scandal. What kind of woman revealed that she relished her senses and her independence, trained her body like an athlete, invited men of letters to her house? What kind of woman wrote and published love poetry? The answer was, according to certain clergymen, and at least one vengeful lover—"a common prostitute." Someone wrote a vulgar ballad about *La Belle Cordière*—"the ropemaker's beautiful wife"—and her name echoed in the streets. There are still people who argue she was a prostitute. Even recently, a girls' high school in Lyon refused to be named in her honor.

Louise had friends who praised her poems loyally, and she tried, for a while, to ignore the publicity, to live with her old bravado. But the prosperity of Lyon had begun to falter, and with it, the fortune of her husband. In 1556, Ennemond Perrin stopped working. Louise retired to the country, to a farmhouse that had been her mother's.

The Renaissance in Lyon was collapsing. Taxes and prices had risen. Jobless and hungry people rioted against the cost of living. There was political tension and religious hatred between Catholics and Protestants.

In 1561, Louise lost her friend Clémence de Bourges, who died from the shock of her fiancé's death in battle. A year later, Lyon was invaded by a Protestant warlord called the Baron des Adrets. There were violent street fights, and the Protestants were victorious.

In 1565, Ennemond Perrin died. We know that Louise continued to live simply and reclusively and that by now she had given up most of her old friends. She made a will the next year, 1566, and died shortly afterward, during an outbreak of the plague. She was forty-four.

X

When I catch sight of your fair head,
garlanded with living laurel,
making your sad lute sound so well
that you compel to rise and be your followers
rocks and trees—when I see you adorned
in virtues legion, paling the brilliant in glory,
chief in honor among men,
then does my passionate heart suppose
that by such virtue as you are beloved,
esteemed by all, so could you love,
and to such worthy virtue could you amend
the virtue of taking pity,
and the virtue of being aroused
sweetly and slowly by my love.

TRANSLATED BY JUDITH THURMAN

XIII

If he folded me in an embrace,
he for whom I live, dying—
if I could share my life's brief space
with him, unharried by all envying,
and if, drawing me to him, he would say: Friend,
let our happiness be each other, swear
no deluge, channel, tempest in the air
shall sever us till our lives end—
and if, then, buckling him to me
as the ivy embraces the tree,
Death, envious, came for me,
or while with kisses we were distracted
my breath from his lips slackened,
I would die happier than I have lived.

TRANSLATED BY JUDITH THURMAN

XXI

What is the height of a great man? How large
is he we venerate? How does his hair
curl or lie straight? And is it dark or fair?
Whose honeyed glance soonest lances the barb
that makes the worse, most hopeless wound to cure?
Whose song most soothes the ear? Whose sadness, sung,
most deeply penetrates? And who among
men draws from the lute a sweetness the most pure?
Whose nature is worthy to adore? I shouldn't wish
to say with perfect certainty. My judgment
has been coached by love. But I know this:
Give me a choice of beauties to admire—
or all the art that works in Nature's name—
they could not, by one flame, brighten my desire.

TRANSLATED BY JUDITH THURMAN

XX

A fortune-teller made the prophecy
that I would love a certain man one day;
her vision was my only portrait of him,
yet I recognized him when I saw him.

Observing, then he loved me fatally,
I pitied his sad, amorous mischance,
and urged my nature on relentlessly,
till I loved with the same extravagance.

You would suppose a passion could only thrive
that fates and gods together did contrive.
But when I see such ominous preparation,

cruel winds stirring to a violent storm,
I think, perhaps, hell sent the invitation,
long ago, to watch my ship go down.

TRANSLATED BY JUDITH THURMAN

VIII

I burn in fire, I drown, I live, I languish,
I feel the heat and cold at both extremes;
Life both brittle and too shapeless seems;
My joy is intermingled with my anguish.
All in an instant do I laugh and cry,
I suffer my grievance as I take my pleasure;
My good life leaves me, and it lasts forever;
All in an instant do I bloom and dry.
Thus Love leads me on inconstantly,
And when I think my sorrow must increase,
I find myself unwittingly at peace.
And when, at last, believing joy at hand,
I stand upon the threshold of my bliss,
He casts me down to where my grief began.

TRANSLATED BY JUDITH THURMAN

XXIII

Alas, what use to me if perfectly
you once sang praises of my golden hair,
and did the beauty of my eyes compare
to twin suns, from which, artfully,
Love shot the darts which caused you so
    much sorrow?
Brief-lived laments, where are you, now?
Where is Death, to whom the honor was due
of your firm love, your often recited vow?
Perhaps you studied to deceive with malice,
enchaining me by feigning loving service?
Forgive me, friend, if for this once I stage
for you my spite, my fury and my outrage.
But then I reassure myself that you,
as much as I, are playing the martyr, too.

TRANSLATED BY JUDITH THURMAN

XVII

In town and temple I'm no longer seen,
Where I was glad to hear your grief confessed,
Where still you can compel me, with no mean
Force, to surrender what we valued best.

I'm bored with masques and tournaments and games,
I can imagine nothing fine but you,
But I endeavor to put out these flames
And change the old desire for something new.

To take my mind off thoughts of love, I stray
Lonely among the loneliest of trees,
But wander as I may, if I'm to be

Delivered from you, then there is no help
For it: I'll have to live outside myself.
Or you to make your home long miles away.

TRANSLATED BY
GRAHAM DUNSTAN MARTIN

II

O sidelong glance, o dazzling dark eyes,
O welling tears, o humid swelling sighs,
O black nights vainly yearned,
O vain bright days returned.
O sad laments, o stubbornest desires,
O sufferings unhinged, o wasted hours,
O deaths in nets a thousand times contained,
O worse evils yet against me framed.
O laugh, o hands, hair, fingers, arms and brow,
O voice, o plaintive lute, viol and bow—
So many torches just to burn a woman.
I accuse you—all the fires you've stolen.
My heart feels after you from town to town;
But not on you the smallest spark has flown.

TRANSLATED BY JUDITH THURMAN

XXIV

Good women, don't reproach me if I have loved,
if I have burned brighter than a thousand flames,
and felt a thousand griefs, a thousand pains,
and if, in weeping, have my days dissolved.

Do not, for this, discredit my good name.
For my past error I reap present sorrow.
Do not hone that sorrow with your blame.
Consider: Love, as easily, tomorrow,

without Vulcan's* fire as an excuse,
without an Adonis† to accuse,
could, at will, change you into a lover

even as I have been, and with less reason,
and make you feel a stranger, stronger passion.
Beware, for more than I, yet may you suffer.

TRANSLATED BY JUDITH THURMAN

---

* *Vulcan*, god of the forge, husband of Venus.
† *Adonis*, exquisitely handsome young mortal with whom Venus fell
in love.

Anne Bradstreet

Make use of what I leave in Love
And God shall blesse you from above.

*T*he poems of Anne Bradstreet—the first poems written in colonial America—give us no glimpse of the strangeness, the savageness, or the beauty of an unsettled country. They don't admit us to the daily life of a woman living on the frontier. They are, instead, as neat, dry, and exotic as if Anne Bradstreet had kept them, like her precious tea leaves, in a tin box. When we open the box, they are even a little musty, like something strong that has been saved for a long time. And yet an exceptional woman is still alive in them.

The great Elizabethan age was still smoldering when Anne Dudley Bradstreet was born, in 1612, the year Shakespeare stopped writing plays. She grew up on a vast estate in Lincolnshire, on England's marshy east coast. Her father, Thomas Dudley, was the steward of that estate, which belonged to the Earl of Lincoln.

Dudley was descended from a noble and very literary family,[17] and he wrote poetry himself, which Anne modeled her early works on. He went to Cambridge University, served as a diplomat, spent his youth in Renaissance high style—as a courtier and scholar. But, in 1597, he converted from the Church of England to Puritanism—a movement in which he was a powerful and sometimes zealous leader. In America, where he held many colonial offices, including that of governor of Massachusetts, Thomas Dudley is remembered as the embodiment of Puritan rigor and Puritan intolerance.

Dudley had married a woman named Dorothy Yorke, "a gentlewoman whose extract and estate were considerable." She seems to have been, in contrast to her husband, a person of patience and tact. Anne Bradstreet had her father's intellectual ferocity. She also had her mother's skill at adapting, at bending, at absorbing hardship.

There was a social distinction between the Dudleys and their employers, but they were close friends just the same. Anne probably shared her lessons with the earl's children. She grew up in a world seasoned by possessions and refinements. She had the library of Sempringham Castle at her disposal, and it seems that she read most of the important writers of her time—Sidney, Spenser, Raleigh, Drayton, du Bartas.[18] She was also steeped in good talk. The people who gathered around Lord Lincoln and her father were courtiers, intellectuals, politicians—and they were passionate for ideas.

All of them had been influenced deeply by the preachings of John Dod, the Puritan minister who had converted Thomas Dudley and many other Anglicans. The Puritans were a sect of Protestants who wanted to reform the Church of England, to scour it of all taint of "Popery"—Roman Catholicism. They had banished the Communion and the Mass from their service; they wanted to dismantle the Anglican hierarchy—its structure of ministers, bishops, and archbishops. They abhorred the pomp, incense, organ music, and sacred art—which the Anglicans had kept despite their break with the Pope's authority. Conscience, not ritual, was the basis of their worship. They felt fervently, sometimes fanatically, that the individual was the caretaker of his or her own salvation. Shoeing a horse, building a wall, stirring a pot, catching a disease, burying a child, taking a walk, making love with one's spouse were all occasions for the Puritans to remember—and to reaffirm—their relationship to God.

Anne's religious education began early. ". . . About six or seven," she wrote, ". . . I began to make conscience of my ways." She read the Bible, and the more she understood, she tells us, "the more solace I took from it." She "knew what was sinfull," but she sometimes gave in to the temptations of "lying, disobedience to parents, etc." When this befell her, she could not rest "till by prayer I had confest it unto God." As she grew up, she struggled with the longings and fantasies that come with adolescence and which were especially shameful and confusing to her. "I found my heart more carnall, and sitting loose from God," she wrote of herself at fourteen. "The vanity and follyes of youth took hold of me."

When, at sixteen, she caught smallpox, she felt it was God's "correction"—his punishment for her daydreams, her self-absorption. With a face budding with sores she "besought the Lord and confessed my pride and vanity and He . . . restored me."

Anne Dudley was married that same year. Her husband was Simon Bradstreet—Thomas Dudley's assistant on the estate. Bradstreet was, like his father-in-law, a graduate of Cambridge University and a talented administrator. He, too, would become a governor of Massachusetts, though not till

many years after Anne's death. He lived to the age of
ninety-three and died an honored statesman.

We know very little of the Bradstreets' courtship and
early life, although their marriage seems to have been a rare
one: a union of ardent friends. We do know that during
their first two years together England was becoming a more
and more dangerous place for Puritans. King Charles had
dissolved Parliament, where the Puritans held a majority.
They were, he felt, not only an obstacle to his extravagance,
but a threat to his power as head of the Church of England.
He hounded or arrested their ministers and the more powerful of their supporters. He exacted "loans" from them,
which they could not refuse to pay.

A small group of Puritans abandoned England and sought
asylum in Holland. Another small group, calling themselves
"Pilgrims," set out in the *Mayflower* and founded a colony
at Plymouth, in Massachusetts. By 1629, with the Earl of
Lincoln a prisoner in the Tower of London, Thomas Dudley
and his friends decided upon the same escape route. They
banded together and agreed to emigrate to America with
their families. They hired ships, engaged artisans, servants,
a doctor, and minister, bought tools, livestock, and provi-
sions and in March of 1630, they set sail.

> *I found a new world and new manners,*
> *at which my heart rose. But after I*
> *was convinced it was the way of God,*
> *I submitted to it and joined to the*
> *Church at Boston.*

Anne Bradstreet was eighteen when the *Arbella* dropped

anchor in Salem harbor. The month was May. The shore smelled "like a garden." A dinghy was launched to give the women "of rank," gentlewomen like Anne and her mother, a taste of land—perhaps to let them gather the wild strawberries growing at high-tide mark.

For two-and-a-half months they had shared a narrow space under the decks with no privacy to be sick, no escape from lice in their hair and clothes. Their food and water had gone bad. Many of the cattle they had providently brought with them were swept overboard during storms.

As winter approached, the colonists found their stores could not be stretched far enough. Anne and her family spent that first winter in a settlement they called Charlestown, which is now part of Boston. They scavenged shellfish from the beach and gathered acorns. The climate, too, was a brutal shock. "Those who had the strength fell to building," Thomas Dudley wrote to the Countess of Lincoln, "but many were interrupted by sickness and died weekly, yea even daily."

After the winter of 1630–1631, the Bradstreet and Dudley families moved to a new village—Newtowne (now, Cambridge). "I fell into a lingering sicknes like a consumption, together with a lamenesse," Anne wrote, "which correction I saw the Lord sent to humble and try me and doe mee Good; and it was not altogether ineffectuall." From that experience came her first poem: "Upon a fit of sickness in her nineteenth year."

While she tried to recover her strength, to "submit" humbly to her new life, and perhaps to work on more poems, Anne was also harboring the grief of being childless. She and Simon had been married for almost five years. Why hadn't she become pregnant? She thought the delay must be another of God's corrections for some shortcoming. "It pleased God to keep me a long time without child, which . . . cost mee many prayers and tears before I obtain one."

Finally, a son, Samuel, was born in 1632, and soon afterward a daughter, Dorothy—after a new move, this time to the village of Ipswich. Sarah followed, and then Simon, and now it must have been difficult to find time for herself. Anne's health was still fragile, and her young children needed strenuous care. She also grew much of her own food, made and repaired clothes, manufactured such supplies as soap, candles, and cloth. In the meanwhile, too, Simon Bradstreet had become a magistrate. He was taking an active part in governing the colony, and he traveled constantly. Anne was often without his company and support.

She wrote doggedly and bravely in those years, in "some few hours curtailed from her sleep and other refreshments"; in moments balanced warily on the edge of danger; or the times when her husband was away, and the wind lisped through the loose fittings of the door. Her poetry seemed to be an escape from all that was wild, unknown, and immediate. The subjects she chose were lofty and historical. She was writing *quaternions:* four books with four parts each. There were four elements, four ages of man, four constitutions, and four ancient monarchies. Anne had borrowed the scheme of "fours" from a poem by her father. She had also been inspired by the style and ambitious range of another Puritan poet—Guillaume du Bartas.

While it was unheard of for a woman to write verse, especially in the philosophical style Anne Bradstreet had chosen, it was a perfectly respectable pastime for Puritan men. Their poems gave form to their struggle to be better Christians. They were occasions for piety and for confession —though not a confession of what we would call "feelings." Very little of that poetry is still readable, including Anne Bradstreet's early efforts. She knitted her lines abstractly, like clothes for a child not born yet, foot after foot of bulky rhymes. But as she developed as a poet, her work would become more than an exercise for her soul. It acquired its own "soul"—whose redemption was being human.

While Anne weeded her garden, counted the heads of her small children, and labored privately and joyfully at her quaternions, Massachusetts Bay was being settled. Political institutions evolved. Nathaniel Ward, a friend of the Bradstreets and an admirer of Anne's poems, drew up "The Body of Liberties"—a basic guarantee of civil rights. A representative democracy was worked out. It was not representative of women, servants, or native Americans, but all "freemen" could vote for the governor and his aides, and could choose delegates to the General Court. Freemen were not necessarily wealthy, or of "gentle" birth, but they had to be members of the Church. Massachusetts was still a Church-State; it didn't tolerate dissent.

Dissent in England—and the king's tyrannical blundering —had, in the meanwhile, forced a crisis. In 1642, the Puritan House of Commons demanded that Charles relinquish his power to them and become a limited constitutional monarch, much like the present queen. When he refused, the English Civil War began.

Anne Bradstreet had grown up on English politics, and

lived at the center of colonial politics, and she followed the war closely. She even wrote a poem about it—"Dialogue Between the Old England and the New"—in which New England, a daughter figure, tries to console and counsel her distraught mother, Old England. But the poem's abstract and sometimes condescending sympathy suggests that Anne, like many colonists had become more American than English—that she felt as distant spiritually as she was physically from the events.

In 1642, ground was broken for a new village on an Indian site that the English had renamed Andover. Simon Bradstreet bought a house-lot of twenty acres and prepared to move his family there. From the records we know he was the first citizen and civil founder of the town. His brother-in-law, the Reverend John Woodbridge, was its religious founder.

At the time of the move to Andover Anne was pregnant with her sixth child and ill with her old "distemper of weakness and fainting." She was also trying to finish the last of her four "monarchies." Perhaps it was now, in the midst of so much change and stress, that she started to write poetry of a different kind—private poems, intended for her husband and family, in which she could tell them her love and plumb her fears for them.

These short and intense lyrics, which were never published in Anne's lifetime, were poems about childbirth, the death of her parents, the fear of her own death. The most intimate of them were about her marriage. Anne wrote to Simon when he went away, when he came home, before she gave birth to their children. She is open about her need for him, and even about their physical love:

> Then while we live, in love let's so persever
> That when we live no more, we may live ever.

The Bradstreets had eight offspring in all—four daughters and four sons. But poetry was Anne's child, too: "my rambling brat" she called it. In "The Author to her Book" she instructs the book: "If for thy father asked, say thou hadst none."

She was, in other words, the only parent of her poems. She alone had given life to them. And they, in turn, had given her a life—a creative life independent of her babies, her famous father, her exhausting housework. It was not an easy second life, either to live or to defend. Creative "enthusiasms" in women were treated harshly by the Puritans, who had already dealt with two such cases—two brilliant women of Anne's age. Anne Hutchinson, a dissenting preacher with many followers, was tried for heresy and expelled to a farm in Connecticut. Anne Hopkins, wife of the governor of Hartford, apparently wrote many books and was considered insane for "giving herself wholly to reading and writing, neglecting her household affairs and meddling in such things as are proper for men."

Anne Bradstreet was more cautious about her writing. She behaved as she was expected to behave as the wife of a magistrate, the governor's daughter, the mother of many children. She accepted being "inferior" in exchange for being tolerated:

Men can do best, and women know it well.
Preeminence in all and each is yours;
Yet grant some small acknowledgment of ours.

Her poetry was, in a sense, licensed by her virtue. Only once, in her poetry, does that virtue defer to a sense of outrage:

I am obnoxious to each carping tongue
Who says my hand a needle better fits . . .
For such despite they cast on female wits:
If what I do prove well, it won't advance
They'll say it's stol'n, or else it was by chance.

Anne's humility helped her survive as a poet, but so did her family's love and sense of her worth. Her father, her husband, and her brother-in-law, acting as "conspirators," took the radical step of making her work public.

In 1647, the Reverend Woodbridge sailed to England on an important political errand. He had also "snatched" the manuscript of Anne's poems, which he trusted to a publisher called Stephen Bowtell. In July of 1649 a small book, costing sixpence, began to appear on London bookstalls. It was called *The Tenth Muse*,[19] *lately sprung up in America, or Severall Poems compiled with great variety of Wit and Learning, full of delight . . . By a gentlewoman in those parts.*

Her name was not on the title page, but several poems in her honor, which introduced her own poems, revealed that she was *Mistris Anne Bradstreet, Vertue's true and lively Patterne, wife of the Worshipful Simon Bradstreet, Esquire,*

At present residing in Occidental parts of the World, in America, alias NOV-ANGLIA.

The publication of *The Tenth Muse* was a double landmark. Anne Bradstreet was not only the first poet of America, she was also the first woman in English literature to publish original verse. To cushion the impact and what seemed like the audacity of that début, the Reverend Woodbridge wrote a friendly and patronizing preface for the book. It was, he promised, the

> Work of a Woman, honoured and esteemed where
> she lives for her gracious demeanor, her
> eminent parts, her pious conversation, her
> Courteous disposition, her exact diligence
> in her place and discreet managing of her
> daily occasions.

He also shielded her modesty by assuring everyone she had taken no part in making the book public—that, indeed, she had resolved "it should never see the Sun."

Anne received her book proudly, although she blushed at the number of printer's errors, at certain awkward phrases, and at references that now embarrassed her. She began to revise them. At the same time she was also working on a new project—a letter to her children, a kind of spiritual autobiography. With the birth of her last child, John, in 1652, she was sick again. If she were to die, she wanted to have recorded her struggles as a Christian, in a form that would be useful to her family.

Her letter explained how her conscience had been formed and changed—first as an earnest child who found it easy to be good, then as a young girl struggling against her senses, then as a pioneer who tried to endure her hardships and losses as God's will, and finally as a woman who reasoned and suffered—who had doubts about God and about the meaning of all her sacrifices for him. Anne's letter didn't offer her children a neat package of maternal wisdom. It offered them herself: a person with many contradictions, a soul "too much in love with the world."

She survived her illness, and her family began growing up. In 1654, her daughter Dorothy married a Boston minister. Her son Samuel had gone to England to study medicine. Simon was admitted to Harvard, the first American university.

At fifty, in 1662, Anne probably had more leisure than she had known since she left England. She began a mellow poem about Nature and God. The New England landscape had lost its terror for her; she had grasped its beauty. She was also compiling a series of aphorisms in prose—another spiritual legacy for her children.

In 1666, the Bradstreet's house in Andover burned to the ground. Samuel Bradstreet recorded that he lost 800 books in the fire. Eight hundred books was an immense library—a measure of how much progress, in terms of leisure time to read—the colony had acquired. Sitting down on a stone, in the charred remains of her living room, Anne Bradstreet must have compared her barren present to her family's first winter in primitive Charlestown, when Thomas Dudley, with no table to lean on, had written his diary on his knees.

The fire destroyed everything that she possessed—all the

weathered and loved things she had moved with and cared for on the frontier. Perhaps Anne wrote these lines leaning on her own knees:

Here stood that trunk, and there
   that chest.
There lay that store I counted best,
My pleasant things in ashes lie.

But Anne was an unshakably faithful woman. God, she felt, had meant her to feel that the home waiting in heaven was better than her earthly one. Perhaps, too, she now felt readier to let go.

At the end of her sixtieth summer, her "old consumption" had left her emaciated. The sight of her arm, pathetically thin, disgusted the woman who was nursing her. But before she died, on September 16, 1672, Samuel Bradstreet promised his mother: "It shall yet be a glorious arm."

The Author to her Book

Thou ill-form'd offspring of my feeble brain,
Who after birth did'st by my side remain,
Till snatcht from thence by friends, less wise than true
Who thee abroad, expos'd to publick view;
Made thee in raggs,* halting to th' press to trudg,
Where errors were not lessened (all may judg)
At thy return my blushing was not small,
My rambling brat (in print) should mother call,
I cast thee by as one unfit for light,
Thy Visage was so irksome in my sight;
Yet being mine own, at length affection would
Thy blemishes amend, if so I could:
I wash'd thy face, but more defects I saw,
And rubbing off a spot, still made a flaw.
I stretcht thy joynts to make thee even feet,
Yet still thou run'st more hobling than is meet;
In better dress to trim thee was my mind,
But nought save home-spun Cloth, i'th' house I find.
In this array, 'mongst Vulgars mayst thou roam
In Criticks hands, beware thou dost not come;

---

* printer's errors

And take thy way where yet thou art not known,
If for thy Father askt, say, thou hadst none:
And for thy Mother, she alas is poor,
Which caus'd her thus to send thee out of door.

To my Dear and loving Husband

If ever two were one, then surely we.
If ever man were lov'd by wife, then thee;
If ever wife was happy in a man,
Compare with me ye women if you can.
I prize thy love more than whole Mines of gold,
Or all the riches that the East doth hold.
My love is such that Rivers cannot quench,
Nor ought but love from thee, give recompence.
Thy love is such I can no way repay,
The heavens reward thee manifold I pray.
Then while we live, in love lets so persever,
That when we live no more, we may live ever.

A Letter to her Husband,
absent upon Publick employment

My head, my heart, mine Eyes, my life, nay more,
My joy, my Magazine of earthly store,
If two be one, as surely thou and I,
How stayest thou there, whilst I at *Ipswich* lye?
So many steps, head from the heart to sever
If but a neck, soon should we be together:
I like the earth this season, mourn in black,
My Sun is gone so far in's Zodiack,
Whom whilst I 'joy'd nor storms, nor frosts I felt,
His warmth such frigid colds did cause to melt.
My chilled limbs now nummed lye forlorn;
Return, return sweet *Sol* from *Capricorn*;
In this dead time, alas, what can I more
Than view those fruits which through thy heat I bore?
Which sweet contentment yield me for a space,
True living Pictures of their Fathers face.
O strange effect! now thou art *Southward* gone,
I weary grow, the tedious day so long;
But when thou *Northward* to me shalt return,
I wish my Sun may never set, but burn
Within the Cancer of my glowing breast,
The welcome house of him my dearest guest.

Where ever, ever stay, and go not thence,
Till natures sad decree shall call thee hence;
Flesh of thy flesh, bone of thy bone,
I here, thou there, yet both but one.

Before the Birth of one of her Children

All things within this fading world hath end,
Adversity doth still our joyes attend;
No tyes so strong, no friends so dear and sweet,
But with deaths parting blow is sure to meet.
The sentence past is most irrevocable,
A common thing, yet oh inevitable;
How soon, my Dear, death may my steps attend,
How soon't may be thy Lot to lose thy friend,
We both are ignorant, yet love bids me
These farewell lines to recommend to thee,
That when that knot's unty'd that made us one,
I may seem thine, who in effect am none.
And if I see not half my dayes that's due,
What nature would, God grant to yours and you;
The many faults that well you know I have,
Let be interr'd in my oblivious grave;
If any worth or virtue were in me,
Let that live freshly in thy memory
And when thou feel'st no grief, as I no harms,

Yet love thy dead, who long lay in thine arms:
And when thy loss shall be repaid with gains
Look to my little babes my dear remains.
And if thou love thy self, or loved'st me
These O protect from step Dames injury.
And if chance to thine eyes shall bring this verse,
With some sad sighs honour my absent Herse;
And kiss this paper for thy loves dear sake,
Who with salt tears this last Farewel did take.

In reference to her Children,
23. June, 1656

I had eight birds hatcht in one nest,
Four Cocks there were, and Hens the rest,
I nurst them up with pain and care,
Nor cost, nor labour did I spare,
Till at the last they felt their wing,
Mounted the Trees, and learn'd to sing;
Chief of the Brood then took his flight,
To Regions far, and left me quite:
My mournful chirps I after send,
Till he return, or I do end,
Leave not thy nest, thy Dam and Sire,
Fly back and sing amidst this Quire.
My second bird did take her flight,
And with her mate flew out of sight;
Southward they both their course did bend,
And Seasons twain they there did spend:
Till after blown by *Southern* gales,
They *Norward* steer'd with filled sayles.
A prettier bird was no where seen,
Along the Beach among the treen.
I have a third of colour white,
On whom I plac'd no small delight;

Coupled with mate loving and true,
Hath also bid her Dam adieu:
And where *Aurora* first appears,
She now hath percht, to spend her years;
One to the Academy flew
To chat among that learned crew:
Ambition moves still in his breast
That he might chant above the rest,
Striving for more than to do well,
That nightingales he might excell.
My fifth, whose down is yet scarce gone
Is 'mongst the shrubs and bushes flown,
And as his wings increase in strength,
On higher boughs he'l pearch at length.
My other three, still with me nest,
Untill they'r grown, then as the rest,
Or here or there, they'l take their flight,
As is ordain'd, so shall they light.
If birds could weep, then would my tears
Let others know what are my fears
Lest this my brood some harm should catch,
And be surpriz'd for want of watch,
Whilst pecking corn, and void of care
They fall un'wares in Fowlers snare:
Or whilst on trees they sit and sing,
Some untoward boy at them do fling:
Or whilst allur'd with bell and glass,
The net be spread, and caught, alas.
Or least by Lime-twigs they be foyl'd,
Or by some greedy hawks be spoyl'd.

O would my young, ye saw my breast,
And knew what thoughts there sadly rest,
Great was my pain when I you bred,
Great was my care, when I you fed,
Long did I keep you soft and warm,
And with my wings kept off all harm,
My cares are more, and fears then ever,
My throbs such now, as 'fore were never:
Alas my birds, you wisdome want,
Of perils you are ignorant,
Oft times in grass, on trees, in flight,
Sore accidents on you may light.
O to your safety have an eye,
So happy may you live and die:
Mean while my dayes in tunes Ile spend,
Till my weak layes with me shall end.
In shady woods I'le sit and sing,
And things that past, to mind I'le bring.
Once young and pleasant, as are you,
But former toyes (no joyes) Adieu.
My age I will not once lament,
But sing, my time so near is spent.
And from the top bough take my flight,
Into a country beyond sight,
Where old ones, instantly grow young,
And there with Seraphims set song:
No seasons cold, nor storms they see;
But spring lasts to eternity,
When each of you shall in your nest
Among your young ones take your rest,

In chirping language, oft them tell,
You had a Dam that lov'd you well,
That did what could be done for young,
And nurst you up till you were strong.
And 'fore she once would let you fly,
She shew'd you joy and misery;
Taught what was good, and what was ill,
What would save life, and what would kill?
Thus gone, amongst you I may live,
And dead, yet speak, and counsel give:
Farewel my birds, farewel adieu,
I happy am, if well with you.

In memory of my dear grand-child
Anne Bradstreet. Who deceased June 20. 1669.
being three years and seven Moneths old

With troubled heart and trembling hand I write,
The Heavens have chang'd to sorrow my delight.
How oft with disappointment have I met,
When I on fading things my hopes have set?
Experience might 'fore this have made me wise,
To value things according to their price:
Was ever stable joy yet found below,
Or perfect bliss without mixture of woe?

I knew she was but as a withering flour,
That's here to day, perhaps gone in an hour;
Like as a bubble, or the brittle glass,
Or like a shadow turning as it was.
More fool then I to look on that was lent,
As if mine own, when thus impermanent.
Farewel dear child, thou ne're shall come to me,
But yet a while, and I shall go to thee;
Mean time my throbbing heart's chear'd up with this
Thou with thy Saviour art in endless bliss.

In memory of my dear grand-child
Elizabeth Bradstreet,
who deceased August, 1665.
being a year and a half old

Farewel dear babe, my hearts too much content,
Farewel sweet babe, the pleasure of mine eye,
Farwel fair flower that for a space was lent,
Then ta'en away unto Eternity.
Blest babe why should I once bewail thy fate,
Or sigh thy dayes so soon were terminate;
Sith thou art setled in an Everlasting state.

2

By nature Trees do rot when they are grown.
And Plumbs and Apples throughly ripe do fall,
And Corn and grass are in their season mown,
And time brings down what is both strong and tall.
But plants new set to be eradicate,
And buds new blown, to have so short a date,
Is by his hand alone that guides nature and fate.

To the Memory of my dear
and ever honoured
Father Thomas Dudley Esq.;
who deceased, July 31. 1653.
and of his Age, 77

EPITAPH

Within this Tomb a Patriot lyes
That was both pious, just and wise,
To Truth a shield, to right a Wall,
To Sectaryes a whip and Maul,
A Magazine of History,
A Prizer of good Company

In manners pleasant and severe
The Good him lov'd, the bad did fear,
And when his time with years was spent
If some rejoyc'd, more did lament.

An Epitaph On my dear and ever
honoured Mother Mrs. Dorothy Dudley,
who deceased Decemb. 27. 1643. and
of her age, 61

    Here lyes,
A Worthy Matron of unspotted life,
A loving Mother and obedient wife,
A friendly Neighbor, pitiful to poor,
Whom oft she fed, and clothed with her store;
To Servants wisely aweful, but yet kind,
And as they did, so they reward did find:
A true Instructer of her Family,
The which she ordered with dexterity.
The publick meetings ever did frequent,
And in her closet constant hours she spent;
Religious in all her words and wayes,
Preparing still for death, till end of dayes:
Of all her Children, Children, liv'd to see,
Then dying, left a blessed memory.

Upon the burning of our house,
July 10th, 1666

In silent night when rest I took,
For sorrow neer I did not look,
I waken'd was with thundring nois
And Piteous shreiks of dreadful voice.
That fearfull sound of fire and fire,
Let no man know is my Desire.

I, starting up, the light did spye,
And to my God my heart did cry
To strengthen me in my Distresse
And not to leave me succourlesse.
Then coming out beheld a space,
The flame consume my dwelling place.

And, when I could no longer look,
I blest his Name that gave and took,
That layd my goods now in the dust:
Yea so it was, and so 'twas just.
It was his own: it was not mine;
Far be it that I should repine.

He might of All justly bereft,
But yet sufficient for us left.
When by the Ruines oft I past,
My sorrowing eyes aside did cast,
And here and there the places spye
Where oft I sate, and long did lye.

Here stood that Trunk, and there that chest;
There lay that store I counted best:
My pleasant things in ashes lye,
And them behold no more shall I.
Under thy roof no guest shall sitt,
Nor at thy Table eat a bitt.

No pleasant tale shall 'ere be told,
Nor things recounted done of old.
No Candle 'ere shall shine in Thee,
Nor bridegroom's voice ere heard shall bee.
In silence ever shalt thou lye;
Adeiu, Adeiu; All's vanity.

Then streight I gin my heart to chide,
And did thy wealth on earth abide?
Didst fix thy hope on mouldring dust,
The arm of flesh didst make thy trust?
Raise up thy thoughts above the skye
That dunghill mists away may flie.

Thou hast an house on high erect
Fram'd by that mighty Architect,
With glory richly furnished,
Stands permanent tho' this bee fled.
It's purchaséd, and paid for too
By him who hath enough to doe.

A Prise so vast as is unknown,
Yet, by his Gift, is made thine own.
There's wealth enough, I need no more;
Farewell my Pelf, farewell my Store.
The world no longer let me Love,
My hope and Treasure lyes Above.

from *The four Seasons of the Year*

SPRING

Now goes the Plow-man to his merry toyle,
He might unloose his winter locked soyl:
The Seeds-man too, doth lavish out his grain,
In hope the more he casts, the more to gain:
The Gardner now superfluous branches lops,
And poles erects for his young clambring hops.
Now digs then sowes his herbs, his flowers and roots
And carefully manures his trees of fruits.

.   .   .

For fruits my Season yields the early Cherry,
The hasty Peas, and wholsome cool Strawberry.
More solid fruits require a longer time,
Each Season hath his fruit, so hath each Clime:
Each man his own peculiar excellence,
But none in all that hath preheminence.
Sweet fragrant Spring, with thy short pittance fly
Let some describe thee better than can I.
Yet above all this priviledg is thine,
Thy dayes still lengthen without least decline.

from *Contemplations*

8

Silent alone, where none or saw, or heard,
In pathless paths I lead my wandring feet,
My humble Eyes to lofty Skyes I rear'd
To sing some Song, my mazed Muse thought meet.
My great Creator I would magnifie,
That nature had, thus decked liberally:
But Ah, and Ah, again, my imbecility!

9

I heard the merry grashopper then sing,
The black clad Cricket, bear a second part,
They kept one tune, and plaid on the same string,
Seeming to glory in their little Art.
Shall Creatures abject, thus their voices raise?
And in their kind resound their makers praise:
Whilst I as mute, can warble forth no higher layes.

18

When I behold the heavens as in their prime,
And then the earth (though old) stil clad in green,
The stones and trees, insensible of time,
Nor age nor wrinkle on their front are seen;
If winter come, and greeness then do fade,
A Spring returns, and they more youthful made;
But Man grows old, lies down, remains where once he's laid.

21

Under the cooling shadow of a stately Elm
Close sate I by a goodly Rivers side,
Where gliding streams the Rocks did overwhelm;
A lonely place, with pleasures dignifi'd.
I once that lov'd the shady woods so well,
Now thought the rivers did the trees excel,
And if the sun would ever shine, there would I dwell.

from *Meditations Divine and morall*

6

The finest bread hath the least bran; the purest hony, the
    least
wax; and the sincerest christian, the least self love.

12

Authority without wisedome is like a heavy axe without an
    edg,
fitter to bruise than polish.

25

An akeing head requires a soft pillow; and a drooping heart
    a strong support.

30

Yellow leaves argue want of sap, and gray haires
want of moisture; so dry and saplesse performances
are simptoms of little spiritall vigor.

Juana Ines de la Cruz

Wisdom is not the know-how
of subtle and vain discourse;
Being wise is knowing only
how to choose: life

*T*he life of Juana Ines de la Cruz is a surprise—as unexpected as if a vine, that should have spread quietly over a rough wall, had suddenly grown stark upright like a tree, lone and magnificent in an open space.

She was born in 1652, in a Mexico that had been living under the Spanish for more than a hundred years. The Spaniards had tried to destroy the culture of the "new" world that they found. In 1569, a Bishop named Landa burned Mayan[20] records of perhaps a thousand years of civilized life—histories, grammars, epics, prophecies, legends, books of medicine, and astronomy—a loss, he noted, which "the Indians regretted to an amazing degree."

In the century that followed, the conquerors settled in. They sent to Spain for wives and built houses for them in the style of the old world, facing inward to the life of courtyards. Their children grew up as Mexicans in name, but Spanish in their way of living. In that tradition women led modest, reverent, and guarded lives. It was not unusual for them to be illiterate. Juana Ines, who came from a Spanish family, sometimes felt her genius was a mistake. "I asked God to put out the light of my intelligence, leaving only enough to keep his law. According to some men, more in a woman is too much—or even dangerous."

(Juana Ines de la Cruz is pronounced: WAH-na ee-NEZ, deh la KROOS)

But for most of her life, mistake or not, she couldn't resist the "vehement impulse to write" and the "continual movement of my imagination." She had, as a tiny girl, discovered the excitement of her own mind. Her mother, Isabel Ramirez de Santillana, couldn't read or write. She never married either of the men with whom she had her six children—Pedro de Asbaje, the father of Juana Ines and her two sisters, and Diego Ruiz Lozano, a farmer.

Asbaje was an adventurer from the Basque country who died or disappeared before Juana Ines could remember him. Her mother, who seems to have been a capable and proud woman, undertook to manage a family estate at Amanameca, a village in the volcanoes, and moved there with her children when Juana was still a baby. The manor house had the library Isabel's father, Don Pedro, had brought from Spain, many of the books underlined in his own hand.

"When I was not yet three," wrote Juana Ines, "my mother was sending my older sister to the local school, where they taught reading. She let me tag along, and listening to the class, the desire to read caught fire in me."

She pretended her mother had promised she could have lessons. The teacher, who wasn't fooled, agreed anyway. "I learned in so short a time I was already reading when my mother found out—for my teacher had kept it secret to increase the pleasure of surprising her with the fact. I, for my part, had said nothing, thinking they would spank me."

That drive to learn was more than ambition or curiosity. It seemed to be as strong as a life process—as the need for nourishment or sleep. "I remember," wrote Juana Ines, "that although I was very greedy as a small child, which is normal at that age, I refused to eat cheese, because I was told it made you stupid, and I was hungrier for knowledge than for food."

When she was seven, she heard there was a university that taught sciences in Mexico City. "I pestered my mother to death, begging her to disguise me as a boy and send me there . . . She wouldn't do it—a good thing—but I avenged my desire to read on the many and various books in my grandfather's library, and no scoldings or punishments were enough to make me stop."

Her grandfather had books of poetry, history, theology, and natural science, but many of them were in Latin, which Juana Ines now decided she would have to learn. Her mother hired a student tutor who gave her about twenty lessons; Juana Ines was so impatient to master everything at once that she cut off six or seven long strands of her hair, and vowed that when they had grown back, if she didn't know what she had promised herself to learn, she would have to cut them again, as a "fine" for her stupidity. "It didn't seem fair that a head be crowned by hair which was so bald of knowledge, an ornament much more desirable."

By the time she was thirteen, Juana Ines was probably running out of books, growing restless in Amanameca, starting to feel impatient with the simple company of her family. Like a tree in a clay pot, she had outgrown her beginnings. Isabel, it seems, understood. She sent her exceptional child to Mexico City to live with an aunt, who had married a nobleman of the court.

Mexico was ruled by a viceroy, a minister of the Spanish king, who was then the Marques de Mancera. Mancera patronized the arts and lived and governed in great splendor.

Her uncle spoke to the viceroy about Juana Ines. What he said—that she could argue logic and theology, had read the classics, could speak Aztec and Latin—must have sounded like folklore, or the rumor of a virgin who worked miracles.

We can picture her audience with Mancera: the viceroy in black, seated in a carved chair under an oval window, listening with astonishment; Juana Ines standing in the light, a slight figure in voluminous skirts, her clear face full of readiness.

Mancera was so impressed he decided to stage a performance for the whole court. He invited a jury of scholars from the university who questioned Juana Ines in all the subjects she professed to know. "She defended herself," the viceroy remarked later, "like a royal galleon assailed by small launches."

That public trial was the first time she could have glimpsed the meaning of her genius—for other people. She saw their looks of wonder. She heard their murmurs of envy. And after her triumph they treated her as a heroine. The viceroy's wife made her a lady-in-waiting and "could not live an instant without her Juana Ines."

Music, banquets, balls, good talk, the novelty of having friends, and their variety—this worldly Mexico drenched her with sensations. But her new glory deepened her sense of being alone—of being unlike all other women:

> with all the applause, I
> succeeded in loving no one,
> being loved by everyone.

She was anxious about her future, too. She had reached

the age when girls were forced to choose between two veils: the white one of the bride, or the black one of the nun. There was no respectable way, in her society, for a woman to live alone.

The choice was bitter for Juana Ines. "There are many things in religious life which repel my character" she wrote. But she also "absolutely rejected marriage." To marry would have meant to lose her freedom to study, and there was nothing that was more important to her. "No censure from others, of which I had a great deal, nor any hesitations of my own, were enough to make me renounce the natural impulse to literature that God put in me."

At fifteen Juana Ines entered a convent, but its routine was too regimented. She tried another convent—San Geronimo—at seventeen. This time she made her vows permanently.

Sister Juana Ines de la Cruz was the "noblest figure in Mexico's colonial poetry."[21] Her thoughts, she says, came to her in meter and rhyme and she had to force herself to write prose.

Most of her poems were written to please others. She wrote in honor of the viceroys, celebrating their birthdays and anniversaries. She wrote plays and songs for the Church, and short drawing-room comedies, in verse, which were performed at court. Her greatest poems were written about love, projecting herself into the voices of different lovers—the sad ones and the jealous ones, the married ones and the betrayed ones, women writing to men and men to women.

If she had a dream to explain, or an idea to develop, she did it in a poem. There is a poem on her theory of harmony and one on architecture. Many of her verses are like pages from a sketchbook, drafts and poses of the same subject in different settings.

Great men wrote to her, and amateurs from all over the world sent her their poems, hoping she would like them. Most of their letters were full of praise and respect. Occasionally they were ironic. A gentleman from Peru sent her a gift of clay cups, suggesting they were magic and could help her become a man. "With me it is not clear," she replied. "Is it a woman you behold? Well, I am not a woman, for I serve no man as a woman."

The standard of living in her convent was not austere. Most of the nuns were from rich families. They lived as they had done at home—ate well, employed servants, received allowances. Juana Ines remained a close friend of succeeding viceroys and was the poet laureate of court life.

Her cell contained a library of 4,000 books and many scientific instruments. From her window she observed the stars. She worked on problems in geometry and physics, painted miniatures, composed baroque music.

But sometimes communal life was noisy and demanding. The sisters loved her and she felt goodwill toward them, but not when they wanted her to gossip, or asked her to settle their petty arguments. She was jealous of her time, hoarding most of it for "reading and more reading . . . studying and more studying." She turned from one subject to another—history, mathematics, astronomy, music, architecture. "I called this one work and that one play. When the pen is still the compass is in motion, the harp gives a rest to the organ."

The torrent of her curiosity never thinned or froze; she never lacked a new idea or a phrase to mold it in. The body of her work amassed—dense and intricate as a snowfall.

And yet, in spite of her genius, her fame, her comfort, her status, her inspiration, it was not easy to be Juana Ines. "Who would not think, hearing the applause, that I have not sailed with the wind behind me on a sea of glass? And yet the Lord knows it has not been thus." She was dogged by critics all her life. Some were envious and mean, but those she could bear. The ones who hurt her most were "those with good intentions, loving me, desiring my welfare, who belittle me by saying 'she affronts sacred ignorance by studying as she does; she will certainly fall from the great height she has reached.' " But she was also kept in check by her own desire to be obedient, to conform, to please. And this impulse sometimes made her ashamed of her genius, like a woman radiantly dressed at a drab party.

I hold in my two hands both eyes
and see only what I touch.

Learning meant seeing, touching, and proving to Juana Ines. She claimed that she was too unworthy to study sacred subjects, but in fact they didn't interest her. Her nature wasn't a mystical or ecstatic one. The Church was suspicious of her love of reason, of her brilliance as a poet and scientist. She was watched closely. And when the authorities judged she had misused her modest freedom, they decided to revoke it.

In 1691, her friend, the Bishop of Puebla, asked her to write down some criticisms she had made on the sermon of a famous priest called Vieyra. He claimed he was eager to see her thoughts on paper—and then, strangely, he published them without her knowledge. Her essay exposed the priest's errors with learned arguments. There was nothing radical about her point of view. If anything it was academic. But when it appeared, it caused an uproar. Who was Juana Ines, a nun, to criticize Vieyra? Her confessor abandoned her. Her friends murmured their dismay. And even the Bishop of Puebla, who had started the trouble, wrote her a suave letter, hiding its abuse beneath friendliness.

> I am not among those who would vulgarly deny women the right to study, but what a shame that such a great intellect has . . . been so debased by lowly observation of the terrestrial.

Juana Ines felt angry, betrayed—but by habit, ashamed, too. She closeted herself for three months to think how she should reply.

That answer, *The Reply to Sister Filotea*,[22] is her masterpiece. It begins carefully and politely—"I don't want any quarrel with the Inquisition,"[23] she wrote. She explains that she had not written poetry in defiance of the Church, but because she had had no choice—it had been forced on her by her own nature.

But then her spirit rises at the unfairness with which she had been judged. "Does being a woman make any difference? Am I not as free to dissent from his opinion as he is from mine? Is my understanding any less free than his?"

This was, in 1691, a revolutionary question. No one believed women could reason, or if they could, that they should devote their lives to it, or if they did, that their ideas should appear in print. For centuries, the Church had frowned on the education of women. Juana Ines found arguments which proved that policy was an error—a mistaken reading of Saint Paul. She pointed to the great women of the Bible—"Deborah, the governor of her people; Judith, the warrior; the Queen of Sheba daring to test her wisdom against the wisdom of the greatest wise men . . ." And she pointed to herself, too. She retold the story of her genius.

Women, she argued, could reason as well as men, and had the same need and the same right to an education. Mothers, she insisted, should be able to teach their daughters—not only sewing and chores—but music, reading, and mathematics. Intelligence, she informed the Bishop, wasn't the privilege of men. There was nothing "masculine" about it:

the greatest understanding is also the most vulnerable.
The greater it is, the more modest and resigned it is,
too, because such understanding is part of the very
being.

When the *Reply to Filotea* was finished, Juana Ines folded her own life as neatly as the blotted letter. She sold her instruments and her books and gave her money to the poor. She turned her friends away. Her cell was empty now, except for three books on sacred subjects, and there she did "violent" penance. "Sister Juana now flies in the way of virtue," her confessor wrote.

This was apparently her own choice. Perhaps it was an act of deference to the Bishop, or to her own spiritual fatigue. Perhaps she thought her sacrifice was proof of her sincerity, that it would give other women a head start.

Three years later, in 1695, there was an outbreak of plague in Mexico City. Juana Ines, nursing the sick, caught the disease and died. She was forty-three.

On Her Portrait

This thing you see, bright ruse
that art, artfully would prove true
with specious reasons of every hue,
is, of the senses, a sly abuse.

By this flattery has striven
to pardon the years of their horrors,
and exempt time of its rigors—
to conquer age and oblivion.

It is only an artifice of the vain,
a brittle flower in the wind,
a shelter futile against being human;

it's a crude offering of devotion,
a work outworn, and looked at well,
a corpse, dust, a shadow, nothing at all.

TRANSLATED BY JUDITH THURMAN

from *A Satirical Romance*

Ignorant men, who disclaim
women with no reason,
you do not see you are the reason
for what you blame.

Importuning her disdain
with such pressing desire,
why is it goodness you then require,
who have caused her shame?

What humor can be so rare
that carelessly will blur
a mirror, and then aver
that it's not clear?

Critics: in your sight
no woman can win:
keep you out, and she's too tight;
she's too loose if you get in.

TRANSLATED BY JUDITH THURMAN

Hope

Jade charm of human life,
mad Hope, gold fever,

dream of the waking, tortuous
as a map of treasure,

ghost of the world, lusting senescence,
decrepit, imaginary vigor;
hourly by the happy expected,
daily by the desperate deferred.

They dog your shade in search of your broad day,
those, who from behind green glass
behold everything tinged by their desire:

may I, with fate more circumspect,
hold in my two hands my two eyes,
see only what I touch.

TRANSLATED BY JUDITH THURMAN

from *Sonnets Of Love and Discretion*

This evening, my love, even as I spoke vainly
to you, beholding how your gestures strayed,
and how the words I spoke failed to persuade,
so I desired you to see my heart plainly.

And to my aid came Love, who took my part,
and willed what by my will had futile seemed:
that in the torrent where my grief streamed
I might, by drops, distil my streaming heart.

Enough harshness, my love, cease and resist
jealousy, even as to a tyrant's torture;
to shadows, rumor, doubts do not give over;
weigh not your peace against such proof as this;

for even as water could you touch and hold
my heart, as through your hands it flowed.

TRANSLATED BY JUDITH THURMAN

I can't hold you and I can't leave you,
and sorting the reasons to leave you or hold you,
I find an intangible one to love you,
and many tangible ones to forgo you.

As you won't change, nor let me forgo you,
I shall give my heart a defense against you,
so that half shall always be armed to abhor you,
though the other half be ready to adore you.

Then if our love, by loving flourish
let it not in endless feuding perish;
let us speak no more in jealousy and suspicion.

He offers not part who would all receive—
so know if that is your intention,
mine shall be to make believe.

TRANSLATED BY JUDITH THURMAN

from *Verses Expressing the Feelings of a Lover*

Lord, beloved,
let my grievances briefly entreat you;
I trusted the wind with them
that they might swiftly reach you—
if only their mournful tone
will not, by that same wind, be blown.

Hear with your eyes
that anguish which your ears
are absent from—those echoes, sighs—
which from my pen arise;
and though my crude voice cannot reach you,
deafly hear what mutely I beseech you.

If you see the amorous stream,
glib lover of wildflowers,
whose sweet tongue does impart the secret,
to all he looks on, of his heart—
then from his current laughter learn to prize
the fluent sorrow of my eyes.

And if the ephemeral flower
and unhumbled rock, which won't consent
to bear time's mark
resemble me, each in its difference,
my joy is that fragility,
and my fastness is that rock.

If you behold the clear sky,
such is the candor of my soul,
and if the day, miserly of its light,
muffles that radiance in gloom,
that darkness and inclemence
mirror my life in this absence.

Thus, loved Fabio
you must pay
no pained attention to my ills,
but learn them freely from the fields,
for they possess my sorrow's measure:
take it, as you take your pleasure.

TRANSLATED BY JUDITH THURMAN

from *In Which Are Described Rationally*
The Irrational Effects of Love

This torment of love
that is in my heart,
I know I feel it
and know not why.

I feel the keen pangs
of a frenzy desired
whose beginning is longing
and end melancholy.

And when I my sorrow
more softly bewail,
I know I am sad
and know not why.

On scant foundations
my sad cares raise
with delusive conceits
a mountain of feeling.

And when that proud mass
falls asunder I find
that the arrogant fabric
was poised on a pin.

In my blindness and folly
I, gladly deceived,
beseech disenchantment
and desire it not.

TRANSLATED BY SAMUEL BECKETT

from *In Which She Fears That Much Learning
Is Useless for Wisdom, and Poisonous
to Real Living*

Let us pretend I'm happy,
for a while, sad Thought;
perhaps you can persuade me—
though I know the contrary.

If my understanding is my own,
truly, why is it then
so quick to dismay me,
and so slow to console me?

Wisdom is not the know-how
of subtle and vain discourse:
being wise is knowing only
how to choose: life

Let us learn, Thought
to be simple, else we shall find
that you have glibly refined us,
and usurped our life's real time.

TRANSLATED BY JUDITH THURMAN

Emily Dickinson

"Til it has loved, no man
or woman can become itself."

$\mathcal{E}$mily Dickinson pretended her life had been "too simple and too stern to embarrass any." If one thinks of that pretence as a play, it needs only the plainest furniture and the squarest little stage. It is set in the middle of the last century, in a New England village. There are many characters, but they are not various—they resemble each other. There are studious women with modest dresses and men with excellent speaking voices. They go to church—all day on Sunday, and bolster their faith at revival meetings. There is a large Labrador dog, an invalid mother who doesn't care for "thought," a clever brother, a devoted, sillyish sister with a temper, a father who is the object of fear and love. The sofas are solid. There are flowers everywhere—branches and bouquets. Once in a while, a lady plays the piano or a gentleman reads aloud from the Springfield *Republican*. Outside, the seasons turn. A Civil War breaks out and ends. There are burials, elections, cattle shows. Bells ring for fire and for the dead. Rye bread rises in the oven. A train passes. A clock is ticking.

Of all the guests who come and go, leaving their cards on the tray, a handful are the main characters in Emily Dickinson's life—but we are not sure who they are. We are not, in fact, sure of who she is, because when she dies— at the end of this quiet play—her sister Vinnie discovers thousands of poems in her dresser drawer. These are the scenes and the rich acts that have taken place invisibly and inaudibly—dyings and lovings, moments of humor and panic, ecstasies, crises of betrayal and despair. This is the fugitive self of perhaps the greatest woman since Sappho to write poetry.

The Emily Dickinson most people think of is the ghostly figure of the older years, when she wore only white, refused to travel farther than her father's grounds, to receive strangers, or sometimes even to see friends. " 'Of shunning men and women—' " she wrote, "they talk of hallowed things aloud and embarrass my dog. He and I don't object to them, if they'll exist their side."

She found her poems among the high reeds of her feelings, in isolated moments which could not have occurred on "their side"—in society, or on a noisy street—which could not have been publicly embraced. Her poems were, as she was, fleeting, camouflaged, alone. When she crossed to her own "side"—to her privacy—and put on her white dress, like a doe's white winter coat, it meant she was in readiness for them.

But as a girl and a young woman, Emily had been very different. She was and remained a passionate friend. She had written the humor column for her school paper, and gushing letters full of gaiety and wit, which often cartooned her family: "Vinnie is snoring! . . . Mother is warming her feet, which she assured me confidently are 'just as cold as ice' . . . Father is really *sober* with excessive satisfaction." She "rode out" with young men, sent valentines, won ryebread baking contests, and she had no small share of vanity: ("I have altered very much since you was here. I am now very tall & wear long dresses nearly.") "The world," she confessed at sixteen, after a trip to Boston, "holds a predominant place in my affections."

That world was a comfortable, conscientious, Yankee one. The Dickinsons were one of the prominent families of Amherst, Massachusetts, where Emily was born on December 10, 1830, the middle of three children. Her father, Edward Dickinson, was a lawyer and a politician who served in Congress, and as the treasurer of Amherst College, which then trained young men for the ministry. He was sternly handsome, with a profile that jutted from a starched collar. His family revered him, although they weren't above keeping secrets from him, or hiding books he disapproved of in the shrubbery, or under the piano cover. He would, Vinnie claimed, have died for any of them, but would never in his life have dreamed of kissing them goodnight.

Emily's mother, whose name was Emily Norcross, was a simple, dependent woman much taken for granted by her family. She was a prisoner of her nerves, was often ill, cranky, probably very lonely. Her husband's political career kept him away from her for long stretches, and her children were witty and alert, which kept them at a distance, too.

When Mrs. Dickinson had a nervous breakdown, Vinnie and Emily became mistresses of the household. Emily resented the chores, especially having to do dishes. "I never had a mother," she wrote later. "I suppose a mother is one to whom you hurry when you are troubled."

She went to school for nine years, the first seven at Amherst Academy, and the final two at Mount Holyoke Female Seminary, in the neighboring village of South Hadley, where she boarded. The seminary atmosphere was ruggedly scholarly and religious. There were courses in Greek and Latin, astronomy, botany, history, singing, rhetoric, physiology, general business, and calisthenics. Many of its graduates became teachers or missionaries. Emily was a brilliant and popular student, the class wit. But she missed her friends from Amherst—the group who had called themselves "The Five" and published a little newspaper. During vacations she wrote long, sentimental letters to them, full of affection and scenery, jokes, gossip, and self-doubt. Much of the doubt was about God and her soul. A Puritan revival was going on, and the girls at Mount Holyoke were urged by their principal, Miss Lyons, to profess "hope," to become Christians in conscience, not only in name. "I regret that last term, when that golden opportunity was mine, that I did not give up and become a Christian," Emily told her friend, Abiah Root. "It is not now too late, so my friends tell me, so my offended conscience whispers, but it is hard for me to give up the world . . ."

It took courage for a young girl to believe herself a "pagan," as Emily did. She never could be sure there was hope of an afterlife, and that uncertainty, that "blank" in her faith, is one of the great themes of her poems.

Emily never inwardly gave the world up, though she retired from its public places as she grew older. Once she finished school, a life took shape for her. It was a life like a fixed star, which rose and set in the same place. There was a trip to Washington with her father, and occasional visits to cousins, and to her eye doctor in Boston, but she moved in tighter and tighter circles until: "I regret to inform you," she wrote to her future sister-in-law, Sue Gilbert, "that at 3 o'clock yesterday my mind came to a stand, and has since then been stationary. Ere this intelligence reaches you, I shall probably be a snail." A year later she told the same correspondent:

> I rise because the sun shines and
> sleep has done with me, and I brush
> my hair and dress me, and wonder that
> I am and who has made me so, and then
> I wash the dishes and anon wash them
> again, and then 'tis afternoon, and
> Ladies call, and evening, and some members
> of another sex come in to spend the hour,
> and then that day is done.

But beneath the sameness, her late twenties and early thirties were years of a terrible inner commotion. She muffled it carefully, except in her poems. Suddenly her creative power had broken loose from her—her poems bounded free as if a spring that had been clenched, were suddenly let go.

Emily Dickinson fell in love, and she seems to have hoped, briefly, for some future with her lover, which never happened. We are not sure who he was, although we think he was her father's friend, the Reverend Charles Wadsworth of Philadelphia, who was married.

She never mentions him by name, and we will never know what occurred, but Emily wrote two love letters to a man she called Master: "Master . . . I can never forget I am not with you . . . open your life wide and take me in . . ."

Sometime in 1861, "Master" drew away from her, and through that year and the next, and the next, we can read the waves of pain traveling outward from the shock inside her. Between 1860 and 1863 she wrote 800 poems, half her life's work, and among them most of the great ones. In her letters, too, her tone is changed. She could still be playful with her friends and send them verses, flowers, a pebble, or a pressed fly. But the center is missing from what she tells them—as if her words were a wreath braided around some loss, an emptiness. "What a privilege it is to be so insignificant!" she writes to her brother's wife. And to a friend:

> Goodnight! I can stay no longer in a world
> of death. Austin is ill of fever. I buried
> my garden last week—Our man Dick lost
> a little girl through scarlet fever . . . Ah!
> dainty Death! Ah! democratic Death! Grasping
> the proudest zinnia from my purple garden—
> Then deep to his bosom the serf's
> child!
>   Say, is he everywhere? Where shall
> I hide my things? Who is alive?

Death was more than just a remote certainty for Emily Dickinson. Women she knew died in childbirth. Babies, children, and young people were swept off by typhoid and other mysterious diseases. The Civil War claimed the lives of boys she had grown up with. She—and everyone in those days—lost an astonishing number of relatives and friends. Death in her poems is also a symbol for any loss, for anything that is irretrievable. Sometimes she sounds alarmed, terrified at the thought of death and its blankness. Sometimes she seems almost grateful she has it to look forward to. She teases herself with the idea, or speaks of death as a familiar friend:

> Because I could not stop for Death—
> He kindly stopped for me—
> The Carriage held but just Ourselves
> And Immortality.

Emily had been writing poetry at least since she was eighteen, and a couple of her poems had been published in the Springfield *Republican*, which was edited by her friend, Sam Bowles. But she had never offered her work to a serious critic, or admitted its magnitude to anyone at all. By her early thirties her poems had ripened, and she must have had an urgent need for someone to taste them and tell her if they were good. In 1862, she read an article in the *Atlantic Monthly* by T. W. Higginson, offering advice to "A Young Contributor" on breaking into print. Higginson was an essayist, a former minister, who was interested in women's rights and in the movement to abolish slavery. He had launched the careers of several women writers. Perhaps for these reasons Emily thought he would be sympathetic. She wrote to him, asking him in the most modest way "to say if my verse is alive."

Higginson was baffled and intrigued by the poems, and by their sender's strange style of address. He asked her for a photograph. Instead of supplying one she told him:

> I am small like the wren, and my hair is

bold, like the chestnut burr; and my eyes
like the sherry in the glass that the guest
leaves. Would this do just as well?

Emily revealed a great deal about herself in her letters to
Colonel Higginson. After her death, her brother Austin sug-
gested Emily had "posed" to the Colonel—but it was just
a face her family had never seen. Perhaps she hoped Higginson would see her poems' rarity—and her own. Yet she was
abjectly grateful even for his most hedging praise. She
signed herself "Your Scholar" and wrote tiny searching
notes to him whenever he failed to respond promptly to her.
"Did I displease you?..."or, on a little card, "Will you in-
struct me then, no more?"

Higginson encouraged her, but he had reservations about
her work, and even doubted her sanity. He describes her to
his wife as "my half-cracked poetess." He tried, for a while,
to lead her poetry "in the direction of rules and tradi-
tions" but she resisted him. She could no more change the
small, tight, oblique shape of her poems than one of her
wildflowers could suddenly produce rosebuds. "I had no
monarch in my life and cannot rule myself," she told
him. "When I try to organize, my little force explodes and
leaves me bare and charred."

He came to visit her because she would not leave Amherst to visit him. She glided into the room on the occasion
of their first meeting in "a very plain and exquisitely clean
white dress, holding two day lilies, which she put in a sort
of childlike way into my hand and said, 'These are my introduction' . . . and added under her breath, 'Forgive me if

I am frightened! I never see strangers' . . ." He told his wife she said things that were "foolish or wise, or that you would have liked: 'Women talk, men are silent. That is why I dread women . . .' 'I find ecstasy in living, the mere sense of living is joy enough . . .' "

He was glad that he didn't live near enough to see Emily Dickinson very often: she drained his nerves more than anyone he had ever met. This was, perhaps, because she admitted so few people to her vivid and private world. Friendships had enormous gravity for her—a gravity that must have been exhausting for those unused to its pull.

Colonel Higginson shared the privilege of reading Emily's poems with someone who was more grateful than he to know them: Helen Hunt Jackson. Mrs. Jackson had met Emily years before when they were both girls in Amherst. She had, since then, launched her own writing career with help from Colonel Higginson, and was a great success. She wrote poetry under the name "H.H." and novels, vignettes, articles, and reviews under the name "Saxe Holm." There was even a rumor, firmly denied by both women, that Helen Jackson and Emily Dickinson had collaborated on some of the Saxe Holm stories.

Unlike Higginson, Helen Hunt Jackson thought Emily was a great poet who should have a public. She begged her to release at least some of her poems—for she guessed there must be many more than she had seen. Emily, alarmed by her friend's persistence, tried to evade her. She did finally grant one small poem, "Success," for an anthology Helen was editing. The poem was published anonymously, and people guessed it was by Ralph Waldo Emerson.[24]

After 1865, Emily's output began to diminish. Her anguish had diminished, too:

> We outgrow love, like other things
> And put it in the drawer—
> Til it an Antique fashion show—
> Like costumes Grandsire wore.

There were other changes in her life. Her father died. Her mother had a stroke and became an invalid. Emily herself had become a complete recluse, a myth in her hometown. She even hid from people she had known for years and cared a great deal for. Vinnie Dickinson and a housekeeper managed domestic affairs and protected Emily from instrusions. Vinnie even had the dressmaker fit her sister's dresses to her own similar figure—to spare her the possible embarrassment of being measured for them.

But Emily wasn't dazed by reality, as her sister thought, even if she recoiled from it. Once they were both wakened by a fire in the middle of the night. A neighbor's barn was burning. Vinnie told Emily not to be afraid, "it's only the fourth of July." "I didn't tell that I saw it," Emily wrote to her cousins, Loo and Fanny Norcross. "I thought that if she felt it best to deceive, it must be that it was . . . I think she will tell us so when we die, to keep us from being afraid."

When Emily was forty-eight, she fell in love a second time—with Otis Lord, a judge of the Massachusetts Supreme Court who was, like Wadsworth, a close friend of her father. She wrote whimsical, ardent letters to Judge Lord, and he, it seems proposed to her. But there were family obstacles to the marriage on both sides, and in 1883, Judge Lord, who was then seventy, died of a stroke.

Her last years were crowded with deaths. Her mother and the Reverend Wadsworth both died in 1882. Emily wrote a stricken letter to Wadsworth's friend, James Clark, asking for the report of his last words. "In an intimacy of many years with the beloved clergyman, I have never before spoken with one who knew him . . . his life was so shy that grief for him seems almost unshared." She also confessed that "I cannot conjecture a world without him."

Helen Hunt Jackson died in 1885, and that same year Emily herself fell ill. The doctors called it "nervous prostration" but she told her cousins, "I feel eternity sweeping around me like the sea."

She stayed in her bedroom, writing at a little table. The room in her house in Amherst is still as it was, spare, fragile, and full of light. There is the black iron stove she fed in winter and kept warm by, a sofa covered in olive velvet, a "sleigh" bed with enormous pillows. She had pictures of George Eliot and Elizabeth Barrett Browning[25] on the wall, and on the windowsill a basket for lowering gingerbread to the neighbors' children.

Emily was suffering from a kidney disease, and by the spring of 1886 she was near death. On May 16, her last day, she wrote her briefest message to Fanny and Loo Norcross:

"Little Cousins—Called Back."

This is my letter to the World
That never wrote to Me—

Emily published only six poems in her lifetime, and she showed only a few more to her friends. But after she died, Vinnie opened her sister's dresser drawer and found a box that contained 900 poems. They were bound together in little "packets"—four, five, or six sheets of folded writing paper stitched through the spine at two points.

These "packets" were her clean copies and her second drafts, in ink, and represented two-thirds of her work. The rest of it was barely legible. Some poems were pencilled in haste on backs of envelopes. They, too, were eventually copied and edited.

Many of Emily's poems are like inspired telegrams: their language is urgent and economical. And sometimes, like telegrams, there is more than one way to read their tidings.

This suspenseful language disturbed Colonel Higginson who had the rather stodgy, formal taste of his times. He believed she was a "wholly new and original poetic genius," but he wasn't willing to admit that she wrote "poetry." There was nothing like her at all—no standard for comparison. When Emily saw him hesitate in the presence of her work, she must have known she could never be understood in her own lifetime:

> I smile when you suggest that I delay
> "to publish"—that being as foreign
> to my thought as Firmament to Fin. If
> Fame belonged to me, I could not escape
> her—if she did not, the longest day
> would pass me on the chase—and the
> approbation of my Dog would forsake me—
> then. My Barefoot-Rank is better.

After her death, when Higginson was editing her book for publication, he changed those words that sounded quaint to him, and smoothed the rhymes that seemed untidy. He also "corrected" her punctuation. What he didn't see was that Emily Dickinson's poems were like the uneven edges of a little key—functional and unique. When her book was published and the key turned, it unlocked the poetry of a new century.

76

Exultation is the going
Of an inland soul to sea,
Past the houses—past the headlands—
Into deep Eternity—

Bred as we, among the mountains,
Can the sailor understand
The divine intoxication
Of the first league out from land?

77

I never hear the word "escape"
Without a quicker blood,
A sudden expectation,
A flying attitude!

I never hear of prisons broad
By soldiers battered down,
But I tug childish at my bars
Only to fail again!

288

I'm Nobody! Who are you?
Are you—Nobody—Too?
Then there's a pair of us?
Don't tell! they'd advertise—you know!

How dreary—to be—Somebody!
How public—like a Frog—
To tell one's name—the livelong June—
To an admiring Bog!

636

The Way I read a Letter's—this—
'Tis first—I lock the Door—
And push it with my fingers—next—
For transport it be sure—

And then I go the furthest off
To counteract a knock—
Then draw my little Letter forth
And slowly pick the lock—

Then—glancing narrow, at the Wall—
And narrow at the floor
For firm Conviction of a Mouse
Not exorcised before—

Peruse how infinite I am
To no one that You—know—
And sigh for lack of Heaven—but not
The Heaven God bestow—

875

I stepped from Plank to Plank
A slow and cautious way
The Stars about my Head I felt
About my Feet the Sea.

I knew not but the next
Would be my final inch—
This gave me that precarious Gait
Some call Experience.

181

I lost a World—the other day!
Has Anybody found?
You'll know it by the Row of Stars
Around its forehead bound.

A Rich man—might not notice it—
Yet—to my frugal Eye,
Of more Esteem than Ducats—
Oh find it—Sir—for me!

664

Of all the Souls that stand create—
I have elected—One—
When Sense from Spirit—files away—
And Subterfuge—is done—
When that which is—and that which was—
Apart—intrinsic—stand—
And this brief Drama in the flesh—
Is shifted—like a Sand—
When Figures show their royal Front—
And Mists—are carved away,
Behold the Atom—I preferred—
To all the lists of Clay!

511

If you were coming in the Fall,
I'd brush the Summer by
With half a smile, and half a spurn,
As Housewives do, a Fly.

If I could see you in a year,
I'd wind the months in balls—
And put them each in separate Drawers
For fear the numbers fuse—

If only Centuries delayed,
I'd count them on my Hand,
Subtracting, till my fingers dropped
Into Van Dieman's Land.*

If certain, when this life was out—
That yours and mine, should be
I'd toss it yonder, like a Rind,
And take Eternity—

But, now, uncertain of the length
Of this, that is between,
It goads me, like the Goblin Bee—
That will not state—its sting.

---

* i.e.: the other side of the world

252

I can wade Grief—
Whole Pools of it—
I'm used to that—
But the least push of Joy
Breaks up my feet—
And I tip—drunken—
Let no Pebble—smile—
'Twas the New Liquor—
That was all!

1765

That Love is all there is,
Is all we know of Love;
It is enough, the freight should be
Proportioned to the groove.

1463

A Route of Evanescence
With a revolving Wheel—
A Resonance of Emerald—
A Rush of Cochineal—
And every Blossom on the Bush
Adjusts its tumbled Head—
The mail from Tunis, Probably,
An easy Morning's Ride—

986

A narrow Fellow in the Grass
Occasionally rides—
You may have met Him—did you not
His notice sudden is—

The Grass divides as with a Comb—
A spotted shaft is seen—
And then it closes at your feet
And opens further on—

He likes a Boggy Acre
A Floor too cool for Corn—
Yet when a Boy, and Barefoot—
I more than once at Noon

Have passed, I thought, a Whip lash
Unbraiding in the Sun
When stooping to secure it
It wrinkled, and was gone—

Several of Nature's People
I know, and they know me—
I feel for them a transport
Of cordiality—

But never met this Fellow
Attended, or alone
Without a tighter breathing
And Zero at the Bone—

585

I like to see it lap the Miles—
And lick the Valleys up—
And stop to feed itself at Tanks—
And then—prodigious step

Around a Pile of Mountains—
And supercilious peer
In Shanties—by the sides of Roads—
And then a Quarry pare

To fit its Ribs
And crawl between
Complaining all the while
In horrid—hooting stanza—
Then chase itself down Hill—

And neigh like Boanerges—
Then—punctual as a Star
Stop—docile and omnipotent
At its own stable door—

436

The Wind—tapped like a tired Man—
And like a Host—"Come in"
I boldly answered—entered then
My Residence within

A Rapid—footless Guest—
To offer whom a Chair
Were as impossible as hand
A Sofa to the Air—

No Bone had He to bind Him—
His Speech was like the Push
Of numerous Humming Birds at once
From a superior Bush—

His Countenance—a Billow—
His Fingers, as He passed
Let go a music—as of tunes
Blown tremulous in Glass—

He visited—still flitting—
Then like a timid Man
Again, He tapped—'twas flurriedly—
And I became alone—

198

An awful Tempest mashed the air—
The clouds were gaunt, and few—
A black—as of a Spectre's Cloak
Hid Heaven and Earth from view.

The creatures chuckled on the Roofs—
And whistled in the air—
And shook their fists—
And gnashed their teeth—
And swung their frenzied hair.

The morning lit—the Birds arose—
The Monster's faded eyes
Turned slowly to his native coast—
And peace—was Paradise!

764

Presentiment—is that long Shadow—on the Lawn—
Indicative that Suns go down—

The notice to the startled Grass
That Darkness—is about to pass—

258

There's a certain Slant of light,
Winter Afternoons—
That oppresses, like the Heft
Of Cathedral Tunes—

Heavenly Hurt, it gives us—
We can find no scar,
But internal difference,
Where the Meanings, are—

None may teach it—Any—
'Tis the Seal Despair—
An imperial affliction
Sent us of the Air—

When it comes, the Landscape listens—
Shadows—hold their breath—
When it goes, 'tis like the Distance
On the look of Death—

465

I heard a Fly buzz—when I died—
The Stillness in the Room
Was like the Stillness in the Air—
Between the Heaves of Storm—

The Eyes around—had wrung them dry—
And breaths were gathering firm
For that last Onset—when the King
Be witnessed—in the Room—

I willed my Keepsakes—Signed away
What portion of me be
Assignable—and then it was
There interposed a Fly—

With Blue—uncertain stumbling Buzz—
Between the light—and me—
And then the Windows failed—and then
I could not see to see—

712

Because I could not stop for Death—
He kindly stopped for me—
The Carriage held but just Ourselves—
And Immortality.

We slowly drove—He knew no haste
And I had put away
My labor and my leisure too,
For His Civility—

We passed the School, where Children strove
At Recess—in the Ring—
We passed the Fields of Gazing Grain—
We passed the Setting Sun—

Or rather—He passed Us—
The Dews drew quivering and chill—
For only Gossamer, my Gown—
My Tippet—only Tulle—

We paused before a House that seemed
A Swelling of the Ground—
The Roof was scarcely visible—
The Cornice—in the Ground—

Since then—'tis Centuries—and yet
Feels shorter than the Day
I first surmised the Horses' Heads
Were toward Eternity—

NOTES

Preface

1. *George Eliot* was the pen name of Mary Ann Evans (1819–1880), one of the greatest English novelists of the nineteenth century.

SAPPHO

2. *Plato* (427–347 B.C.) was a famous Greek philosopher, disciple of Socrates (c. 469–399 B.C.), and teacher of Aristotle (384–322 B.C.). Socrates attracted a school of followers—young men whom he taught to think by a method of question and answer (Socratic dialogue).

3. *Aesop*, author of *Aesop's Fables*, was a deformed slave. *Jeremiah*, one of the major prophets of the Jews, predicted they would be taken captive by *Nebuchadnezzar, the King of Babylon.*
Solon, ruler of Athens, was a great lawgiver and sage.

4. Pittecus

5. Paul Roche, from the Introduction to *The Love Songs of Sappho,* © 1966, The New American Library

6. Aristotle, see note 2.

7. Another famous woman, *Corinna* of Thebes, supposedly taught the poet Pindar.

8. *The Muses* in Greek mythology were the nine daughters of Zeus and Mnemosyne. Each one was the patron of an art or science: *Calliope*—the muse of epic poetry; *Clio*—the muse of history; *Erato*—the muse of love poetry; *Euterpe*—the muse of lyric poetry; *Melpomene*—the muse of tragedy; *Polyhymnia*—the muse of sacred poetry; *Terpsichore*—the muse of choral song; *Thalia*—the muse of comedy; *Urania*—the muse of astronomy.

Several women poets have received the title "The Tenth Muse," including Juana Ines de la Cruz and Anne Bradstreet.

A muse is also someone—traditionally a woman—who inspires an artist's work.

9. C. B. Bowra, *Greek Lyric Poetry*, Oxford, 1936

9a. Aphrodite was not just a symbolic figure. The gods and godesses were real to the Greeks of the sixth century. Sappho probably believed Aphrodite had real power over her passions. Her hymn to the godess is one of her few poems we possess intact.

10. Denys Page, *Sappho and Alcaeus*, Oxford, 1955

11. Socrates, see note 2.

12. Mary Barnard, *Sappho, A New Translation*, Univ. of Calif. 1958

13. The *Leucadian Cliffs* were a limestone ridge on the island of Leucas, in the Ionian Sea. Every year, the Leucadians sacrificed some guilty person to Apollo. They threw him from the cliffs—but not before they had attached all sorts of live birds to his shoulders and back, whose fluttering could help break the fall. Below, in the sea, a crowd would gather in small boats to retrieve the victim, and ferry him to safety.

14. The *Aeolians*, an ethnic group, were the inhabitants of the northern part of the Aegian coast, including the island people of Lesbos and Tenedos.

14a. See note 12.

LOUISE LABÉ

15. *Perpignan* was a fortified town in France very near the Spanish border. The battle, between the French and Spanish, was to control it.

16. The greatest of these other poets was *Pierre Ronsard* (1525–1585), a nobleman and court poet for Henry II and Charles IX. He and his friends called themselves The *Pléiade*—after the Pleiades, a constellation of seven stars which, according to Greek mythology, were supposed to have been seven goddesses.

A *Pleiad* is a name that is sometimes given to a circle of illustrious persons.

ANNE BRADSTREET

17. Dudley was related, through his mother, to the *Sidneys*, a noble family whose most brilliant member was Sir Philip Sidney, poet, scholar, soldier, and courtier—the model of a Renaissance man. Sir Philip's sister Mary, Countess of Pembroke, was a distinguished scholar and translator. Anne was aware and proud she had that "selfsame blood in my veins."

18. Adrienne Rich, from the foreword to *The Works of Anne Bradstreet*, Belknap Press, Harvard Univ., 1967

19. The Tenth Muse, see note 8.

JUANA INES DE LA CRUZ

20. The *Mayans* were a native American people who built one of the world's greatest civilizations in parts of Mexico and Central America. Their culture dated back to 1000 B.C. and perhaps before.

21. according to *Octavio Paz*, Mexico's leading contemporary poet.

22. The Bishop wrote to Juana Ines using the pen name of an imaginary nun: the sister *Filotea*. Juana Ines knew perfectly well who had written the Letter—but she kept up the pretense, and replied to "Filotea," rather than to the "Bishop."

23. The *Inquisition* was a religious court, also called The Holy Office, set up to investigate crimes against the Roman Catholic religion. It was very powerful, especially in Spain, between 1237 and 1820. Torture was used as a means of extracting evidence and/or confessions.

EMILY DICKINSON

24. *Ralph Waldo Emerson* (1803–1882) was an American poet and essayist, a figure of great influence and prestige in nineteenth-century literature.

25. *Elizabeth Barrett Browning* (1806–1861) was an English poet and author of love sonnets.

    George Eliot, see note 1.